How to Pool Risks across Generations

UEHIRO SERIES IN PRACTICAL ETHICS

General Editor
Julian Savulescu, University of Oxford

How to Pool Risks across Generations

The Case for Collective Pensions

MICHAEL OTSUKA

OXFORD
UNIVERSITY PRESS

Great Clarendon Street, Oxford, OX2 6DP,
United Kingdom

Oxford University Press is a department of the University of Oxford.
It furthers the University's objective of excellence in research, scholarship,
and education by publishing worldwide. Oxford is a registered trade mark of
Oxford University Press in the UK and in certain other countries

Published in the United States of America by Oxford University Press
198 Madison Avenue, New York, NY 10016, United States of America

British Library Cataloguing in Publication Data

Data available

Library of Congress Control Number: 2023933408

ISBN 978-0-19-888596-2

DOI: 10.1093/oso/9780198885962.001.0001

Printed and bound by
CPI Group (UK) Ltd, Croydon, CR0 4YY

Contents

Acknowledgements

Chapters 1–3 of this book are revised versions of three Uehiro Lectures in Practical Ethics which I delivered in November 2020. I thank the Oxford Uehiro Centre for Practical Ethics and its Director Julian Savulescu for their invitation to deliver, and their hosting of, these lectures. I'm grateful to the Uehiro Foundation on Ethics and Education for their generous sponsorship.

Material from Chapter 1 was also presented at the Third International Seminar on Supplementary Pensions, Brasília, in December 2021 and the New York University Center for Bioethics in October 2022; a version of Chapter 2 was presented at the University of Reading in November 2020; and versions of Chapter 3 were presented at the LSE and Oxford in January 2018, the Université catholique de Louvain in March 2020, the Institute for Futures Studies in March 2022, and the Hebrew University in April 2022. Owing to the Covid pandemic, the events from November 2020 to April 2022 were online.

For their written comments on drafts of the chapters of this book, I am very grateful to James Franklin-Adams, Matthew Arends, Nicholas Barr, Philip Bennett, Michael Bromwich, Paul Dixon, Catherine Donnelly, Alexander Douglas, Simon Eagle, Luna Fadayel, Alon Harel, Joseph Heath, Adam Hofri, Robert Jubb, Con Keating, Larry Locke, Bastian Steuwer, Alex Voorhoeve, Kevin Wesbroom, Paul Willetts, and two readers for Oxford University Press.

In 2021–22 I had the privilege of serving as an alternate member of the Joint Negotiating Committee (JNC) of the Universities Superannuation Scheme (USS), by appointment of the University and College Union (UCU). I owe a great debt to my union colleagues inside and outside of the JNC for shaping my understanding over the years of the issues that figure in this book. My understanding of USS was also enriched by the papers that USS officials prepared for JNC meetings and by discussion with USS officials and employer-appointed members of the JNC.

Some of the material in Chapter 2 has been published, in somewhat different form, in Michael Otsuka, 'Does the Universities Superannuation Scheme Provide a Model of Reciprocity Between Generations?', *LSE Public Policy Review* 2 (2021): 1–6. © Michael Otsuka under the terms of the Creative Commons Attribution 4.0 licence. DOI: 10.31389/lseppr.42.

Material drawn from the Introduction, Chapter 4, and the Conclusion will be published, in slightly modified and abridged form, in sections II–IV of Michael Otsuka, 'Fair Terms of Social Cooperation among Equals', *Journal of Practical Ethics* (in press).

Chapter 4 is a revised version of sections 4–6 of Michael Otsuka, 'How to Guard against the Risk of Living Too Long: The Case for Collective Pensions', in David Sobel, Peter Vallentyne, and Steven Wall, eds., *Oxford Studies in Political Philosophy*, vol. III (Oxford University Press, 2017), pp. 229–51, https://global.oup.com/academic/product/oxford-studies-in-political-philosophy-volume-3-9780198801238. Some of the material in sections 1–3 of that article has been incorporated, in revised form, into other chapters of this book. These have been reproduced by permission of Oxford University Press.

Introduction

The welfare state serves not only to relieve poverty and otherwise redistribute from rich to poor, which Nicholas Barr has described as its Robin Hood function. It also serves to pool our risks through social insurance, in a manner that is to the expected advantage of each. When 'considering the combined effects of taxes and benefit', Barr has estimated that 'between two-thirds and three-quarters of welfare-state spending [in the UK] is self-financed'—which is to say non-redistributive.[1] Both of these aims of the welfare state—poverty relief through redistribution from rich to poor and mutually advantageous insurance against risk—are present in the provision of pensions, which is the topic of this book.

Through the transfer of income from the middle to the later years of our lives, pensions provide a solution to the problem we would otherwise face of living so long that we find ourselves lacking sufficient resources to sustain ourselves and prosper throughout retirement. This solution is realized through the continual transfer of the fruits of the labour of those who are relatively young, healthy, and able-bodied to those who are elderly, no longer in work, and often infirm, in a manner that involves cooperation over the life cycles of overlapping generations.

Should these transfers be conceived and defended as the redistribution of resources between distinct individuals to eliminate unchosen misfortune? There are compelling reasons, grounded in a commitment to fairness in the way things turn out, for the state to relieve poverty in

---

[1] Barr, *The Economics of the Welfare State*, p. 180. Barr maintains that this range is 'not out of line with the experience of other high-income countries' (ibid.). To take one example, Paul Krugman has declared that 'the U.S. government is…best thought of as a giant insurance company with an army. When you talk about federal spending, you're overwhelmingly talking about Social Security, Medicare, Medicaid, and defense' ('An Insurance Company with an Army').

How to Pool Risks across Generations: The Case for Collective Pensions. Michael Otsuka, Oxford University Press.
© Michael Otsuka 2023. DOI: 10.1093/oso/9780198885962.003.0001

old age by redistributing from those who are known to have had greater fortune in accumulating wealth during their lifetimes, to others who are known to have had less good fortune. Such reasons are implied by 'luck egalitarian' theories which political philosophers such as Ronald Dworkin and G. A. Cohen have identified with justice.[2]

Or should these transfers be conceived and defended as a form of cooperation between persons which is to the expected benefit of each? On this different understanding, a failure to provide pensions collectively would be condemned in large part as irrational because inefficient and wasteful, rather than being condemned as a breach of a duty to alleviate the unchosen misfortune of those who are known to be badly off. These considerations can ground a reciprocity-based defence of pensions as constituting fair terms of social cooperation for mutual advantage, which are the terms that John Rawls has identified with justice.[3]

In this book, I consider the extent to which two different types of pension can be justified as a realization of reciprocity: the first involves funding, whereas the second is provided on an unfunded 'pay as you go' (PAYG) basis. With PAYG, the pensions of retired workers are paid for by the contemporaneous contributions of current workers. In a funded pension, by contrast, the pensions of retired workers are paid for by their own previous contributions and those of their employers during their time in work, along with subsequent investment returns.

In the first two chapters of this book, I draw attention to the ways in which funded pensions involve *intra*personal transfers from one's more fortunate to one's less fortunate self, where these selves can be understood either temporally or modally. On a temporal understanding, there is a consumption-smoothing transfer of resources from one's young, healthy, and productive self to one's elderly, infirm, and unemployable self. On a modal understanding, there is a transfer of resources between different possible retirements one might end up experiencing, from those in which one's annual income would otherwise be high to those in which this income would otherwise be low. These transfers are to each person's

---

[2] See Dworkin, *Sovereign Virtue*, and Cohen, *Rescuing Justice and Equality*. See also Chapter 4, n. 8, and my account of luck egalitarianism in 'Equality, Ambition, and Insurance'.
[3] In addition to my discussion of Rawls in Chapters 3 and 4, see the opening section of Otsuka, 'Fair Terms of Social Cooperation among Equals'.

expected advantage, which is made possible by a fair sharing of the fruits of social cooperation which arise through the efficiencies reaped by the pooling of the risk of outliving what one could save for one's retirement on one's own.

Throughout this book, I set out the case for the collective provision of pensions on grounds of reciprocity rather than redistribution. I do so, not out of any denial of the soundness of a redistributive case for pensions. Those who are impoverished in old age, through no choice or fault of theirs, are entitled to pensions as a matter of egalitarian justice. Even when their impoverishment can be attributed to past choices for which they can be held responsible, they might still be entitled to pensions as an upshot of their equal claim to worldly resources.[4] Rather, I appeal to grounds of reciprocity because I think a strong case for collective pensions remains, even in the absence of grounds for redistribution from rich to poor. As Barr has written: 'Even if all poverty and social exclusion could be eliminated, so that the entire population were middle class, there would still be a need for institutions to enable people to insure themselves and to redistribute over the life cycle.'[5] There would, for example, remain a case for the collective provision of occupational pensions, which will form the main focus of this book. Such provision would be justified by virtue of the fact that the risk sharing of such arrangements is to the expected advantage of each.

In the parlance that now prevails, funded occupational pensions are divided into two types: 'defined contribution' (DC) and 'defined benefit' (DB). With DC, one's entitlement is specified ('defined') solely in terms of the level of contributions during one's working career into a fund earmarked for one's retirement. For example, it might be spelled out that, so long as a worker contributes 5% of her salary into the pension fund each year, her employer will match and double that with a 10% contribution. DC does not provide an entitlement to any level of pension income in retirement. Rather, such income will depend on how one's contributions are invested and how well these investments turn out.

---

[4] For a spelling out of the nature and grounds for such a claim, see Otsuka, *Libertarianism without Inequality*, ch. 1, and 'Appropriating Lockean Appropriation'.

[5] *The Welfare State as Piggy Bank*, p. 1.

With DB, by contrast, one's entitlement is specified in terms of a level of pension income (i.e., 'benefit') in retirement. It might be spelled out, for example, that one will receive 1/80th of one's final salary for every year that one has been a contributing member of the pension scheme.[6]

In a typical DC arrangement, one bears the risk of living so long that one spends one's last years on earth in poverty because one has outlived the savings in one's own private 'pension pot' that have been invested for one's retirement. This predicament has famously been described by a Nobel laureate in economics as the 'nastiest, hardest problem in finance'.[7] This risk can be mitigated through an arrangement known as a tontine, whereby the assets of those who die earlier are redistributed to those who manage to outlive them. Tontines were once widespread in Europe and the USA but have become historical relics that now survive mainly as fictional murder plots in film and cartoon. In Chapter 1, I show how the tontine provides an elegant theoretical basis for increasingly collective solutions—involving the pooling of risks associated with longevity and investment returns—to the aforementioned nasty problem. These solutions fall under the banner of 'collective defined contribution' (CDC). In one variant of CDC, the risks are collectively pooled only among the members of each age cohort. In another form, they are collectively pooled across different cohorts. In this chapter, I explicate the promising design of a version of the latter that Royal Mail is introducing for its members.

All forms of CDC involve a collective pooling of longevity and investment risk among workers, in the manner of a mutual association. With funded occupational DB pensions, in contrast to CDC, such risk is borne, at least directly, by the sponsoring employers rather than their workers. This gives rise to the problem of how to ensure that employers will be able to deliver the benefit they have promised, which is typically an inflation-protected income in retirement until death, specified as a fraction of the salary earned during one's career. In Chapter 2, I consider the concepts and principles, within and beyond financial economics, that underlie the regulation, valuation, and investment of such DB schemes in

---

[6] As I explain in Chapter 3, DB pensions need not be funded. They might also take an unfunded or notionally funded PAYG form.
[7] See Ritholtz, 'Tackling the "Nastiest, Hardest Problem in Finance"'.

order to provide such assurance. I assess the merits of the 'actuarial approach' to funding an open, ongoing DB pension scheme at a low rate of contributions invested for the long term in 'growth assets' such as equities (stocks and shares) and property. I also consider the merits of the contrasting 'financial economics approach', which calls for a higher rate of contributions set as the cost of purchasing government and corporate bonds that 'match' the liabilities by providing guaranteed streams of income that closely approximate the promised pension payments. I show how the UK's large, multi-employer Universities Superannuation Scheme (USS) provides a model for the actuarial approach. The 'last man standing' mutuality of this scheme constitutes a reciprocity-based prototype for the delivery of DB pensions across society more generally, involving the collective pooling of risks across geographic space as well as over succeeding generations. Such an arrangement justifies the actuarial approach to the funding of DB over the financial economics approach.

On any sensible approach to the valuation of a funded DB scheme, ineliminable risk will remain that returns on a portfolio weighted towards growth assets will fall significantly short of fully funding pension promises. On the actuarial approach, this risk is deemed sufficiently low that it is reasonable and prudent for open, ongoing schemes with strong employer sponsors to take. But if the risk is so low, shouldn't scheme members who advocate such an approach be willing to put their money where their mouth is, by agreeing to bear at least some of this downside risk through a reduction in their pensions if returns are insufficient to achieve full funding?

I argue across Chapters 1 and 2 that some such conditionality would simply involve a return to the practices of DB pension schemes during their heyday three and more decades ago. The subsequent hardening of the pension promise into an unconditional guarantee has hastened the demise of DB by rendering it unaffordable. The best has become the enemy of the good. The target pensions of CDC, which I discuss in Chapter 1, provide a means of reaping most of the benefits of collective pensions, in a manner that is more cost effective than that of a funded DB pension whose promise is underwritten by a bond portfolio.

Chapters 1 and 2 grapple with the problems that funded collective pension schemes face. In Chapter 3, I ask whether an unfunded pay as you go approach might provide a solution. With PAYG, money is directly transferred from those who are currently working to pay the pensions of those who are currently retired. Rather than drawing from a pension fund consisting of a portfolio of financial assets, these pensions are paid out of the state treasury's coffers. I explore the extent to which a PAYG pension can be justified as a form of indirect reciprocity that cascades down generations. I consider the claim that a PAYG arrangement in which each generation pays the pensions of the previous generation can be justified as in mutually advantageous strategic equilibrium. I conclude by making the case that reciprocity can be realized by a notionally funded PAYG scheme, of which the UK Teachers' Pension Scheme provides an example.

In this book, I show how all three of the approaches considered across Chapters 1–3—CDC, DB, and PAYG—converge on a similar form of collective pension provision, which breaks open the silos of individual DC pension pots while avoiding the high expense of funding that is pegged to bond yields. Whether it ultimately takes the form of a notionally funded PAYG DB scheme, a genuinely funded DB scheme, or CDC, we should adopt a collective, multigenerational, society-wide form of pension provision.[8]

The Rawlsian idea of fair terms of cooperation for mutual advantage figures prominently in the case I make for collective pensions. These terms involve the cooperation over the life cycles of overlapping generations, by the sustenance of those at the end of their lives through the fruits of the labour of those in the middle of their lives. In Chapter 4, I explain how such pensions can provide fair terms of cooperation that respect both the freedom and the equality of different members of society over time. I also explain how such pensions can help to realize the Rawlsian ideal of a property-owning democracy.[9]

---

[8] This book also includes an Appendix, in which I ask what relation, if any, one's pension, and one's contributions towards it, should bear to one's salary. I answer this question from both the standpoint of the rational self-interest of the worker who receives the pension and the standpoint of fairness between persons among other impartial considerations of public policy.

[9] It was, in fact, through my thinking about pensions that I finally came to see the force of Rawls's approach to social justice, and to relinquish much of my prior commitment to a contrasting luck egalitarian version of left-libertarianism which I defended in *Libertarianism without Inequality*.

Throughout this book, normative and philosophical claims of a general and theoretical nature emerge from discussion of actuarial, financial, and regulatory considerations that are grounded in concrete historical and contemporary practices, institutions, and rules. I hope to show that philosophers have something to contribute to the assessment of the valuation and design of pensions. In addition to providing a reciprocity-based justification of collective pensions involving fair terms of cooperation for mutual advantage, philosophers can play a role in identifying conceptual confusion regarding the nature and purpose of a valuation of a pension scheme. They can also expose the unsoundness of implicit assumptions regarding the nature of a bond, the stringency of a promissory obligation, freedom of choice, and the demands of intergenerational fairness. These and other matters should not be left solely to actuaries, financial economists, regulators, and other pensions professionals. A broader perspective is salutary.[10]

I shall now turn, in the opening chapter, to a consideration of a stripped-down, highly atomized, individualistic form of pension provision. This will help to isolate the different challenges we face in providing for our old age and the range of solutions available. From this individualistic starting point, I will build up, within and across the chapters, to increasingly collective forms of pension provision. In so doing, I hope to clarify the workings and functions of the various integrated parts of collective pension schemes. We shall see that there is an interesting range of possibilities that lie between starkly individualistic and highly collectivistic forms of pension provision: different degrees and forms of collectivization in which risks are pooled to an increasing degree.

---

[10] As I record in my acknowledgements, I am, however, heavily indebted to a number of people whose knowledge of the intricacies of actuarial practices, pensions regulation, institutional design, finance, or the history of UK pensions far exceeds my own. I could not have written this book without their expertise, which has been informed by practices and disciplines beyond my own.

1
The Case for Collective Defined Contribution

As its title indicates, this is a book about how collectives pool risks across generations in order to provide pensions. Yet pension provision is not necessarily intergenerational or social in nature. It can arise even if we restrict ourselves to a single generation and, within that generation, a single, isolated individual. Here the problem of how to provide for one's old age would be especially acute. We can imagine a Robinson-Crusoe-like character stranded alone on a desert island, who knows that she will never be rescued. Although she is now capable of roaming the island to gather food to sustain herself, she realizes that infirmities will eventually set in and force her to retire to a more sedentary life. She knows she will die of starvation if she does not make provision, while she is mobile and active, for sustenance in her old age.

In striving to provide for her retirement, she faces two risks that render pension provision difficult for all of us: longevity risk and investment risk. Her longevity risk is that of not knowing how long she will live in a condition of infirmity in which she is no longer able to roam the island to gather food. On the one hand, she wants to make sure that she has made enough provisions to consume so that they last as long as she would live in this infirm state, to the point when she would die of something other than starvation. On the other hand, she wants to make sure she does not expend unnecessary time and labour making provisions that will outlast her and go to waste after she dies. In grappling with what we can describe as her investment risk, she will need to decide what foods to gather based on her knowledge of how well they will keep before they spoil. We can also imagine that she has choices involving positive returns on investment, such as the planting of a garden that will continue to bear nearby fruit when she is no longer able to roam, or,

How to Pool Risks across Generations: The Case for Collective Pensions. Michael Otsuka, Oxford University Press.

more fancifully, the fermenting of drinks that will improve with age during her retirement.

Under an increasingly prevalent means of pension provision in contemporary societies, many will attempt to cope with longevity and investment risk on their own in a manner that does not radically depart from my desert island vignette. What I'm referring to is the familiar and increasingly common individual defined contribution (IDC) retirement savings plan, which works roughly as follows.[1] You, and typically also your employer, make monthly contributions into your 'pension pot' during your working years. These contributions are typically set as a fixed percentage of your income. You decide how to invest these savings. When you retire, you make use of what you have accumulated to provide yourself with income in retirement. Increasingly, people choose to do so by drawing down their funds, by means of withdrawals from a continually invested pot until it is depleted.[2]

Such a practice of income drawdown involves significant exposure to longevity risk. If you knew exactly how long you would live in retirement, you could budget to cover precisely that number of years. But one typically does not know the date of one's death. Rather, one is limited to statistical knowledge of the life expectancies of people who are similarly situated. If, for example, you are a British man who has just reached the age of 66, which renders one eligible for a full state pension, your mean life expectancy is nineteen more years, to the age of 85. However, you have a one-in-four chance of living seven more years beyond, to the age of 92, and a one-in-ten chance of living to 96. If you are a 66-year-old British *woman*, your mean life expectancy is twenty-one more years, to the age of 87. However, you have a one-in-four chance of living to 94 and a one-in-ten chance of living to 98.[3]

---

[1] In the USA, the most common of these is known as a '401(k)', named after a subsection of the Internal Revenue Code that provides tax relief for such a plan.

[2] Both here and in my desert island vignette, I am using the term 'pension' somewhat expansively to refer to income in retirement, even if that involves nothing other than the drawing down of one's own savings.

[3] These figures are taken from the life expectancy calculator of the UK's Office for National Statistics: https://www.ons.gov.uk/peoplepopulationandcommunity/healthandsocialcare/healthandlifeexpectancies/articles/lifeexpectancycalculator/2019-06-07. They are roughly comparable to the life expectancies across different OECD countries, though mean life expectancy is somewhat longer, by about one or two years, than those figures that apply to the USA.

Suppose that you are a British woman who has chosen to retire at the age of 66, and you are in possession of no information that would differentiate your prospects from those of any other 66-year-old woman. How should you decide what proportion of your pot to draw down each year? Should you assume that you will live the mean number of twenty-one more years, and therefore divide your pension pot into twenty-one equal parts, one for each year? If you do that, there's a greater than 50% chance that you will deplete your pension pot before you die, since the median number of years a 66-year-old will live is somewhat higher than the mean number of years.[4] In order to ensure a very high, 90% chance that you will have a regular income until death, you will need to divide your pot into thirty-two equal parts, one for each year until the age of 98. If you do that, however, you will run a very high chance that you will not be able to take full advantage of your pension pot during your lifetime. It is difficult to manage the dual and competing risks of your money running out before you die and of having left much of your pot unconsumed at death.

Even if you happen to know precisely how long you will live in retirement—let us assume that you know you will live exactly twenty-one more years—you are faced with the further problem that it will be difficult to divide your pot into twenty-one equal portions unless you invest it very conservatively. First, the equality of the portions should be in real rather than nominal terms, which is to say that they should be equal once one adjusts for any decline in purchasing power due to inflation. One would need to invest in inflation-index-linked bonds or derivatives that hedge against inflation to facilitate a division into twenty-one parts that are equal in real terms. Second, investments with high expected return are purchased at the cost of exposure to the risk of unpredictable variability of outcome. Therefore, unless you invest conservatively in a manner that simply hedges against inflation, it will be impossible to know how much to withdraw each year, to ensure that you receive equal income in real terms throughout the rest of your known lifespan. On account of these difficulties, the financial economist and Nobel laureate William Sharpe has described income drawdown as the

---

[4] Spiegelhalter, 'Why "Life Expectancy" Is a Misleading Summary of Survival'.

'nastiest, hardest problem in finance'.[5] It is, however, a problem that increasing numbers of retired individuals in the UK, the USA, and elsewhere face on their own, as defined contribution pension pots become more and more prevalent, as does income drawdown as the means of transforming these pots into retirement income.

In this chapter, I shall consider the workings and merits of a promising solution to this 'nastiest, hardest problem in finance', which bears the name of 'collective defined contribution' (CDC) and will soon be provided to postal workers for Royal Mail. Under the different name of a 'variable annuity', a similar form of pension has been on offer for several decades to American university teachers and researchers enrolled in the Teachers Insurance and Annuity Association of America's College Retirement Equities Fund (TIAA-CREF).[6] They are based on the simple idea that it is possible to limit the employer's liability to nothing more than a set contribution (a 'defined contribution' or DC), while, at the same time, retaining many of the benefits of the pooling of risks of a traditional defined benefit (DB) occupational pension scheme, which are absent from IDC. These risk-pooling arrangements, whose mechanisms I shall describe below, are thought to make it possible to invest CDC pension contributions largely in growth assets such as equities and property, as was once the norm for DB pensions. Proponents of CDC maintain that such a scheme would safely and reliably deliver pensions to members that are superior to the provisions of IDC, without exposing employers to the risks involved with the underwriting of more traditional DB pensions liabilities. They regard it as the solution to the challenge of providing a generous, reliable, and affordable pension income from retirement to death.

In order to provide a point of reference for CDC, and a benchmark of comparison, I shall begin with a sketch of the manner in which individuals with DC pension pots have addressed the problems of longevity and investment risk in the past. It was once more common for an individual to enter into the following market exchange with an insurance company at or near the point of retirement. One agrees to transfer the assets one

---

[5] Ritholtz, 'Tackling the "Nastiest, Hardest Problem in Finance"'.
[6] See n. 20 of this chapter.

has accumulated in one's pension pot to an insurance company. In exchange, the insurance company provides one with an annuity: the guarantee of a steady stream of income from retirement until death, with or without increases to partially or fully cover price inflation.[7] One thereby transfers all longevity and investment risk to the insurance company.

Here is how the insurance company is able to handle longevity risk much more effectively than a single individual can. As I mentioned earlier, for someone in the UK who now retires at the full state pension age of 66, one's average life expectancy is about twenty more years: nineteen for a man, twenty-one for a woman. No individual who begins to draw down one's own pension pot upon retirement can safely assume that one will live the average number of years. For all one knows, one might live anywhere from one to forty years beyond date of retirement. As I noted earlier, this uncertainty makes it difficult for an individual to plan and budget for income drawdown. By the law of large numbers, however, an insurance company which writes annuities for a great many individuals of the same age who are retiring at the same time can safely assume that the different lifespans will average out to something very close to twenty years. This figure is statistically stable, with a low degree of variance, when applied to a large population, in a manner that facilitates precise budgeting.

That is how an insurance company handles longevity risk. Here is how it handles the investment risk of funding an annuity in exchange for a retired worker's pension pot. An insurance company is required by solvency regulations to have sufficient capital to ensure that it has a 99.5% chance of paying out the promised annuity.[8] To achieve this level

---

[7] Like an annuity, a DB pension promises a steady stream of income from retirement until death, which may involve increases to partially or fully cover price inflation. The main difference between such a DB promise and an annuity is that the level of retirement income provided by the former is typically determined by the number of years a member has contributed into the scheme during her working life, whereas it is determined by the value of the lump sum of cash transferred to the insurance company in the case of the latter.

[8] An insurance company receives large sums of money up front from buyers when it sells annuities. But what the buyers receive in return are small streams of income spread out many years into the future. Hence, such a capital requirement is deemed necessary as collateral to prevent unscrupulous insurance companies from declaring bankruptcy and defaulting on these future obligations once they've received the cash up front.

of certainty, it invests in financial assets that 'match the liabilities' by providing streams of cash flows that are equivalent to those of a promised pension, in their magnitude and duration and the certainty that they will be delivered. These consist largely of high-quality corporate bonds, long-dated, inflation-linked government bonds, and other fixed-income assets. It is for this reason that the cost of an annuity tracks government bond yields fairly closely. Since these yields have been extremely low in recent years, the cost of an annuity has also recently been very high.

While it is possible, in the manner I have just described, for an individual to eliminate investment and longevity risk by means of purchase of an annuity in exchange for one's pension pot at or near point of retirement, such a person is faced with the following two significant financial risks leading *up* to retirement. First, an individual has no control over what the relevant bond yield, and therefore the rate at which one can convert one's pension pot into an annuity, will be at point of retirement. In fact, day-to-day fluctuations in bond yields can make a significant difference to the rate at which one is able to convert one's pension pot into an annuity.[9]

In addition to the rate at which one can convert the assets in one's pension pot into an annuity, the overall size of one's pot at point of retirement will make a difference to the adequacy and generosity of the annuity one will be able to purchase. In order to try to maximize the value of assets at point of retirement, pension pots are typically invested mainly in growth assets such as equities and property, which have higher expected returns than bonds, throughout most of the working lives of DC pot holders. On account, however, of the greater variance of returns on growth assets than those of bonds, and the lack of correlation of returns on the former with the latter, DC pension pots are typically sent, by default, on a 'life cycle' path of de-risking out of equities and property into bonds during the years leading up to retirement. One rationale for such a shift is to protect against a great fall in the value of growth assets, from which it will be difficult to recover, close to the point at which one

---

[9] See Merton, 'The Crisis in Retirement Planning'.

will need to exchange these assets for an annuity.[10] A further rationale is that greater investment in bonds provides an effective hedge against an increase in the price of the purchase of an annuity at retirement, since that price is determined by the price of bonds in which annuity providers invest. Historically, however, such an investment strategy would have been a costly and ineffective form of protection against risk for both British and American workers. According to one study, in the vast majority of years from 1948 to 2007, this sort of life-cycle de-risking would have made workers in the UK and the USA poorer in retirement than if they had maintained a high-wire strategy of remaining invested purely in equities throughout their career.[11]

In comparison with the collective nature of a traditional DB pension scheme that is the topic of Chapter 2, a worker with his own DC pension pot should be regarded as a pension scheme consisting of a single member. Within at most a few decades, his working life and his life itself will come to an end. This is for the simple reason that the 'days of our years *are* threescore years and ten; and if by reason of strength *they be* fourscore years, yet *is* their strength labour and sorrow; for it is soon cut off, and we fly away'.[12] When he retires, an individual's one-person pension fund will stop receiving any further contributions into it, along the lines of the collective pension fund of a sponsoring employer who ceases trading. If he would like a guaranteed pension income for life, he will need to arrange for the assets of his pension scheme to be 'bought out' by an insurance company that provides a bond-backed annuity in exchange, as described earlier. As also noted earlier, such an individual will feel pressure to de-risk his pension fund from stocks to bonds during the years leading up to retirement.

Might there be a more cost-effective way for an individual to manage longevity and investment risk than by means of life-cycle de-risking during the decade or so leading up to retirement, followed by

---

[10] If, for example, someone had been entirely invested in UK equities and had retired on 24 March 2020, rather than 20 February 2020, that person would have had assets worth 33% less, with which to purchase an annuity on date of retirement. But a fund offered to UK academics involving life-cycle de-risking would have declined by only 9% in value during that period.

[11] See Figure 1 in Cannon and Tonks, 'The Value and Risk of Defined Contribution Pension Schemes', p. 106.

[12] Psalms 90:10.

insurance company buy-out? The answer is 'Yes'. The solution involves collectivization into a mutual association for mutual advantage. Unlike the traditional employer-sponsored DB pension plan which is the topic of the next chapter, this association involves just *workers* who band together. Employers do not share in the underwriting of the risk.

Here is one promising collective solution, which operates largely within—and involves only minor modification of—the familiar structures of IDC pension pots.[13] Rather than expensively de-risking their portfolios during the years leading up to retirement, at which point they purchase an annuity whose income is pegged to the yield on bonds, individuals keep their pension pots continuously invested throughout their working lives in a portfolio heavily weighted towards growth assets with higher expected returns. When an individual reaches retirement age, he and others who retire at the same age and date enter into the following income drawdown arrangement with one another. The average life expectancy of these members in retirement is computed. Let us assume that this is twenty years. These individuals hire an actuary to provide them with a best estimate of the long-term returns of their pension pots over the next twenty years. The actuary also calculates how much could be withdrawn each month from the pension pots of each retired member, such that if the expected long-term returns on investments were precisely realized each year, and an equal amount[14] were withdrawn from the fund each month, then the entire pot would be completely depleted after exactly twenty years. Each individual would receive these equal amounts in the form of income drawn down from the fund, directly proportional to the size of his pension pot at time of retirement.

We haven't yet solved the problem with income drawdown mentioned earlier, that some individuals will live longer than the rates at which their pension pots are drawn down and others will die before their pots are completely depleted. The solution involves the introduction of the following vital twist. For anyone who dies before twenty years have elapsed,

---

[13] For a discussion of a range of such solutions, see Donnelly, 'Pooling Pensioners' Resources'.

[14] Equal in real (inflation-adjusted) terms rather than nominal terms.

the assets he would have received between his death and his twentieth year of retirement are redistributed to the pension pots of everyone else in his cohort who remains alive, to be drawn down by them in the event that they live more than twenty years. This process is iterated, so that, for anyone who dies after twenty years have elapsed, his unconsumed assets are also redistributed to the pension pots of those who will live longer. Eventually, all the assets are redistributed so that they are drawn down by the last person alive. Unlike the so-called 'last man standing' multi-employer pension arrangement which will be the topic of the next chapter, this is literally a last 'man' standing arrangement.

The pension scheme I have just described is essentially a version of an arrangement known as a tontine, which traces its origins to Europe in the seventeenth century, was widespread in the eighteenth and the nine-teenth centuries, and played an especially large role in providing for the retirement of people in the USA at the turn of the twentieth century.[15] Unlike many of the historical instances, which involved a transaction with an insurance company or a government, the version of a tontine I've just sketched takes the form of a mutual association. In the case of ordinary individual income drawdown, assets in one's pension pot that one has not consumed at one's death go to one's heirs or whomever one designates in one's will. Under this tontine arrangement, by contrast, the assets go to everyone else in one's cohort who belongs to the same mutual association, in a manner that provides insurance against the risk of outliving one's own pension pot.[16]

Although I have just explained how such a tontine handles longevity risk, I have not yet explained how it handles investment risk. Given the volatility and uncertainty of returns on growth assets, the expected long-term returns on such assets will not be precisely realized. Therefore, a tontine runs the risk of either drawing down growth assets too quickly, so that the long-lived members of the cohort that form the mutual

---

[15] 'It's estimated that by 1905, there were 9 million tontine policies active in a nation of only 18 million households' (Guo, 'It's Sleazy, It's Totally Illegal').

[16] Many historical instances of tontines did not involve such drawdown of capital. Rather, they consisted of coupon bonds issued by an insurance company or the government, whose principal was never paid back. When someone died, the coupon payments on his bonds were transferred to survivors, until the point when there were no more survivors, with no repayment of the principal.

association outlive them, or else drawing down the assets too slowly, so that some of them go to waste by remaining on the table unconsumed after all members of the association die. Such investment risk can be managed by means of life-cycle de-risking. But, unlike the life-cycle de-risking referred to earlier, which takes place during the last decade of the working lives of scheme members, here de-risking out of growth assets and into bonds would begin only at point of retirement. The portfolios of the cohort that forms a tontine would gradually de-risk during the retirement years of the members until all that remains is a bond portfolio shared by only those who are unusually long-lived.

Under an innovative arrangement along these lines that Royal Mail has proposed, complete de-risking into a low-risk bond portfolio is achieved only at the point at which members of the cohort have reached the age of 90. An actuary for Royal Mail has estimated that such an arrangement can be expected to give rise to an average level of pension income for people who retire now, which would be 70% greater than the income they would have received if they had de-risked, in more traditional fashion, from a growth portfolio into a bond portfolio during the last decade of their working life and purchased an annuity upon retirement.[17] The reason why expected pension income is so much greater during retirement has entirely to do with the fact that the portfolios of members remain entirely invested in growth assets for longer. It all comes down to the difference between the dashed line and the solid line in Fig. 1.1. The dashed line represents returns on a pension pot for someone who de-risks in traditional life-cycle fashion to purchase an annuity at retirement. Its initial high horizontal placement represents expected long-term returns on a growth portfolio, of slightly less than 4% above the yield on long-dated government bonds (the so-called risk-free rate). The initial drop in the dashed line represents the decade long de-risking during the years leading up to retirement. The further drop down to the low dashed horizonal line represents the income from a guaranteed inflation-linked annuity, when benchmarked against the yield on long-dated government bonds. By contrast, the solid line represents the

---

[17] See Willis Towers Watson, 'Analysis: How CDC Pension Levels Compare with Other Types of Schemes'.

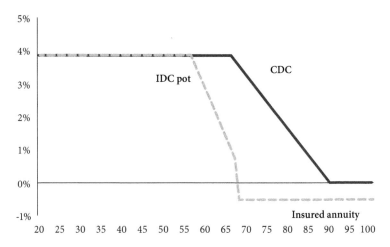

Fig. 1.1 Comparison of expected returns on investment approach for an IDC annuity versus CDC (or similarly invested tontine or CIDC)

Source: Willis Towers Watson, 'Analysis: How CDC Pension Levels Compare with Other Types of Schemes', p. 3.

high returns on a growth portfolio in which scheme members are invested until the point of retirement, and then a gradual de-risking descent to a pure bond portfolio by the time any scheme members reach the age of 90.

The absence of de-risking before retirement increases expected pension income by about 15% in comparison with an annuity, and the returns on investment in growth assets during retirement increases expected income in retirement by a further 50%. The two increases compound to a 70% overall improvement, relative to the de-risking involved in the purchase an annuity.[18] This figure represents the amount of improvement one can expect *on average* over a guaranteed annuity income. Depending on how returns on growth assets actually turn out, relative to bonds, what people end up receiving in retirement might be

---

[18] Willis Towers Watson, 'Analysis', p. 3. The finding that CDC on average delivers better outcomes than annuity purchase, and the Royal Mail design that tapers investment risk in a manner that tracks each member's age, each stem originally from research by Aon. See Wesbroom et al., 'The Case for Collective DC', p. 30, and Arends et al., 'Collective DC—Stability and Fairness', p. 4.

more or less than a 70% improvement on the guaranteed income from an annuity.[19]

In the case of any cohort that retires in a given year and enters into a tontine arrangement, the solid line also represent the *expected* returns on their pension pots before and during retirement. Especially during the period in which people are invested entirely in growth assets, the actual returns of cohorts of different ages that retire in different years might vary quite a bit. To reduce this variability and unpredictability of income depending on date of retirement, different cohorts might agree in advance to smooth over the higher or lower returns on investments of the cohorts that retire in different years. If the returns of the pension pots of a given cohort exceed the expected mean represented by the solid line, those higher-than-expected returns would be transferred to the pension pots of those cohorts whose returns fall short of the solid line. As a result, different cohorts would receive an income closer to that which is implied by the solid line than they would have if each cohort had internalized all their gains and losses, with no transfer from cohorts with good investment luck to those with bad investment luck.

With the introduction of this smoothing of investment returns between the different cohorts that enter into tontine arrangements, we have now arrived at a description of the workings of Royal Mail's proposed new CDC pension scheme.[20] With its absence of such smoothing of returns between different cohorts, the tontine arrangement I described earlier is a variant of CDC known as CIDC, or 'collective individual defined contribution'.

One of the virtues of the Royal Mail scheme is a feature of its design which makes it possible to provide generous pensions even if the scheme

---

[19] As noted earlier, however, the guaranteed level of annuity income is locked in only at point of annuity purchase at retirement. This level will vary depending on how well investments in one's pension pot have fared leading up to retirement and on prevailing bond yields and therefore annuity rates when one retires.

[20] As I noted earlier in this chapter, TIAA-CREF offers American university teachers and researchers a similar arrangement known as a 'variable annuity'. Like Royal Mail's CDC, it relies on the mechanism of the tontine to manage longevity and mortality risk during retirement, in a manner that pools risks across cohorts. The main difference with Royal Mail is that individuals are provided with choices regarding their level of investment risk in TIAA-CREF, whereas all are invested in the same manner (as described in the main text of this chapter) in the case of Royal Mail. See Barr and Diamond, *Better Pension Design*.

closes to the entry of new members and slowly goes into runoff as existing members retire and then die. Here the arrangement would gradually transform from CDC to CIDC. Absent the influx of new members into the scheme, we will eventually arrive at the last cohort of workers who retire as scheme members. This last cohort and those immediately preceding them will be treated as self-standing tontine arrangements which I initially described, with no cross-subsidy or smoothing between the different cohorts. Hence, the scheme will eventually resolve itself into a pure version of CIDC. It will be possible for these final cohorts to stand on their own bottoms, given the gradual de-risking of their portfolios, which I described earlier, and which is represented by the downwardly sloping solid line. In the absence of smoothing across different cohorts, there will be more variability in pension income, depending on year of retirement. But the gradual de-risking of the portfolios, combined with the redistribution from the dead to the living of the tontine mechanism, will still render it likely that most members of a given cohort will receive a relatively predictable and steady income until death, which is much more generous than the guaranteed income in retirement one could purchase in the form of an annuity from an insurance company. The longest-lived, last-standing members of a given cohort will, however, be faced with an increasingly unpredictable and unstable level of pension promise.[21]

One could avoid these problems of increased variability in the income of members as the scheme winds down, by keeping it open for the long term, with a large and steady influx of new members. If one could be confident that the scheme would remain open for the foreseeable future spanning several more decades, with at least a one-for-one replacement of retiring members with new members, then one would not need to introduce a gradual de-risking of the portfolios of members in retirement. Rather, one could remain indefinitely invested in a high level of growth assets—as one would always have the option of smoothing differences in returns between different cohorts—in order to provide everyone with the level of pension income which is implied by the expected return on these growth assets. Here we introduce smoothing,

---

[21] See Bernhardt and Donnelly, 'Quantifying the Trade-off'.

not just between all existing members of the scheme as in the case of Royal Mail, but also between existing and anticipated future members of the scheme.

CDC schemes that smooth investment risk across different cohorts in this manner have been subject to a charge of intergenerational unfairness. It has been argued, for example, that 'the first generation in CDC gets a free ride. It may receive a payment from the second generation, without risking paying an earlier generation'.[22] This charge misfires. Such smoothing is fair both to different generations and to the young in comparison with the old. While it is true that the first generation bears no risk of having to subsidize an earlier generation, this is balanced by the fact that they have no prospect of receiving a subsidy from an earlier generation. Risks and prospects of gain are also symmetrical when we compare the first generation with subsequent generations. Assuming that each generation's pension pay-out is based on a best estimate of the median return on their investment, there is a 50% chance that the plan will be overfunded during one's retirement, and a 50% chance that it will be underfunded. If it is underfunded, pensions will be paid in part out of the contributions of younger workers. But the positive flipside of this liability to subsidize the pensions of their elders is the 50% chance that their elders will leave them with a surplus to protect them against shortfalls, relative to this best estimate, in the funding of their own pensions. Therefore, the risk pooling is shared equally between the first and subsequent generations. The smoothing favours the unlucky over the lucky, irrespective of their age or the generation to which they belong.[23] By contrast, the unfairness of the differential investment luck depending on one's year of retirement is not mitigated at all in the case of the CIDC tontine arrangement described earlier, on account of its lack of any smoothing between different cohorts.

When the pooling of risks applies across future as well as present members of a scheme, we will have arrived—by building up from IDC through the addition of different forms of risk pooling—at a pension

---

[22] Ralfe, 'Collective Defined Pensions Are a "Ponzi Con Trick"'.

[23] For an explanation of how it can be rational for a later generation to enter a CDC pension scheme even if it is underfunded at the time, see Cui et al., 'Intergenerational Risk Sharing', p. 3.

scheme very much like the traditional funded employer-sponsored DB pension schemes as they existed in the UK until roughly the end of the twentieth century. It was common for such schemes to be funded on the basis of a best estimate of returns on a portfolio constantly invested heavily in growth assets, perhaps with an 80% weighting towards equities. Such an investment approach can be approximated by a horizontal line that runs across Fig. 1.1 at the level of roughly 3% returns over the risk-free rate. An 80% equities portfolio is not as heavily invested in growth assets as the pre-retirement portfolio of Royal Mail. For that reason, the horizontal line would be lower than the horizontal pre-retirement portion of the solid line, where returns are roughly 4% above the risk-free rate. But, unlike the solid line, there is no de-risking of the assets that corresponded to the retirement years of individual members. Hence there is no downward sloping of the line. It remains horizontal at about 3% above the risk-free rate, during both the pre-retirement and the retirement years of each worker in the scheme. The justification for this absence of de-risking is that, even though individuals will age and die, the scheme as a whole will remain 'evergreen', as the average age of members remains relatively unchanged, through the influx of new members to replace those who retire. It will, therefore, always remain possible to smooth differences in investment returns across different cohorts.

When, as in the case of Royal Mail's CDC, a pension scheme encompasses only those workers employed by a single company, it will rarely be safe to assume that this firm will remain solvent for the indefinite future, with a workforce undiminished in size.[24] Hence it will be unsafe to assume that the scheme will remain evergreen. Rather, one will need to ensure that the scheme is robust to closure to new members, in the manner that Royal Mail has done, as described above. In the next chapter, I shall explain how it is possible, through the banding together of many different companies into a large multi-employer scheme, to

---

[24] Royal Mail has suffered from the technological shift from posted letters to online communication. While it delivered 20 billion letters a year two decades ago, today it delivers only 8 billion letters a year. With the accompanying rise in online shopping, its business model has shifted to the delivery of parcels, where it is in competition with other large parcel delivery firms to retain its share of this market. See Jordan, 'Royal Mail to axe up to 10,000 jobs'.

ensure that a collective pension scheme will remain open for the indefinite future, with a large and steady influx of new members. I shall consider and build upon the example of the Universities Superannuation Scheme (USS), which unites multiple university employers across the UK into a single pension scheme. At the limit, such an arrangement could extend across the entire economy, encompassing all workers in a given society, rather than just those within a single firm or multi-employer occupational group.

I shall close this chapter by making the following philosophical case for the sort of evergreen pension scheme arrangement described in the previous paragraphs. By joining together as collectives in the manner famously depicted on the frontispiece of Hobbes's *Leviathan*, it is possible to tame the risks we would face as individuals, each with our own private pension pot. A collective pension can be justified as a 'social union of social unions', to borrow a phrase from John Rawls.[25] Each first-order social union is created by a set of covenants that unites the members of a cohort who will retire at the same time into the mutual association of a tontine arrangement. Such covenants are to the mutual benefit of each, as they pool and tame the longevity and investment risks that each faces as an individual. The different cohorts in turn will find it rational to enter into covenants with one another in order to pool and smooth over the investment risks that remain. Those cohorts whose invested contributions exceed the expected growth rate agree to transfer to cohorts whose investments fall short, in a manner which smooths over investment risks, and allows constant investment in higher-risk growth assets with higher expected return. Investment risk is tamed by each cohort in the scheme's entering into covenants with other cohorts, thereby binding them together into a multigenerational corporate body.

Such a funded pension scheme should be conceived of as an enduring collective entity, which is formed by the agreements of different individuals to pool risks, in a manner that involves reciprocity between the different individuals who constitute the collective. The multigenerational corporate body that arises from a collective pension scheme is 'an

---

[25] *A Theory of Justice*, §79.

ongoing entity with a long-time horizon'.[26] Given realistic assumptions, it can remain continually invested in higher-risk assets with higher expected returns, in order to provide each of the individuals who constitute this collective a better pension than she could hope to generate through her own personal DC pension pot.

We can therefore conceive of the case for collective pension provision as a form of reciprocity involving cooperation between persons for mutual advantage. Investment and longevity risk are pooled through the insurance of a mutual association, in a manner which is to the *ex ante* advantage of each. This is achieved by the transfer of resources, not simply between different people, but also within the possible future lives of each individual: from one's more fortunate possible future selves to one's less fortunate possible future selves.

---

[26] See Brown and McInnes, 'Shifting Public Sector DB Plans to DC', pp. 23, 17.

2

The Case for a Funded Pension with a Defined Benefit

Since the global financial crisis of 2007–08, there has been a dramatic fall in the number of open defined benefit (DB) pension schemes in the UK. In 2006, there were 3.6 million British workers enrolled in such schemes in the private sector that were open to their accrual of further pension promises in their years leading up to retirement. By 2021, that figure had dropped to just below 1 million. Of those, only about two thirds were in pension schemes that were also open to the enrolment of new members.[1] About 30% of those in such fully open DB schemes were members of a single one: the Universities Superannuation Scheme (USS).

USS provides a case study for this chapter. It provides pensions for workers in the roughly seventy UK universities that were founded from medieval times through to the late 1960s, plus the roughly seventy Oxford and Cambridge colleges. USS offers an illustration of what has gone wrong with the measurement and regulation of pension risks in recent years and the role this has played in the decline of DB. It also points the way to how these risks might be more sensibly managed in the future, in a manner that involves the reciprocity and risk pooling within and across generations which I described at the close of the previous chapter.

USS was, in fact, founded in 1975 to mitigate the risks to which university teachers had been exposed in the defined contribution (DC) scheme that pre-dated it. That scheme had been criticized for the lack of a predictable relation between one's salary at retirement and the pension one could obtain by means of annuity purchase. For the reasons discussed in the previous chapter, members with the same length of service

---

[1] Pension Protection Fund, *The Purple Book*, pp. 4, 10.

How to Pool Risks across Generations: The Case for Collective Pensions. Michael Otsuka, Oxford University Press. © Michael Otsuka 2023. DOI: 10.1093/oso/9780198885962.003.0003

and retiring salary ended up receiving very different levels of pension income depending on their date of retirement. These DC pensions were also criticized for falling short of the inflation-indexed, final salary DB pensions that civil servants and schoolteachers in the public sector received.

When it was introduced nearly fifty years ago, USS offered the prospect of a solution to these problems with the DC scheme it replaced. Rather than their having to wait and see how much their pension pots had grown and what the annuity rate would be at date of retirement, USS promised to pay each member an income from retirement to death that bore a predictable relation to one's final salary of 1/80th of that salary for each year that one had contributed to the scheme. Members also received full protection of this pension against erosion by inflation during retirement.[2] This level of promise was modelled on the public sector pensions provided to civil servants and schoolteachers at the time. Consequently, in exchange for an initial modest increase in contributions, USS offered what was widely regarded as a superior pension to what one could realistically expect under its DC predecessor. Members were given the option of remaining in the DC scheme, but they almost universally transferred into USS.[3]

For the ensuing three decades spanning 1975–2016, USS continued to provide 1/80th final salary pension promises to members already in the scheme, in exchange for a relatively modest though increasing level of annual contributions. USS has not, however, been immune from the pressures that have given rise to the dramatic fall across the UK in the membership of open DB schemes, as outlined in the opening paragraph of this chapter. The scheme has been in a perpetual state of crisis in recent years, with every valuation from 2011 to 2020 giving rise to one or both of a reduction of the DB pension promise and an increase in the level of contributions. In 2018 the DB scheme was nearly forced to close entirely to both new members and future accrual.

---

[2] In addition, members were entitled to a lump sum on retirement, equal to three times their pension.
[3] Drawing on Logan's *Birth of a Pension Scheme*, I provide a fuller account of the DC predecessor to, and the foundation of, USS in 'Does the Universities Superannuation Scheme Provide a Model of Reciprocity?'

An examination of how USS was valued in the mid-1990s, in contrast to how it was recently valued in 2020, will shed light on both the recent decline of USS and the demise of DB in the UK more generally. These two valuations also provide concrete practical illustrations of competing schools of thought regarding the proper valuation and funding of a DB pension scheme. They show how the intellectual theories of actuaries and economists employed by universities and consultancies can have profound real-world consequences.

The method the scheme actuary employed to value USS in 1996 was little different from the way this and other final salary DB schemes had been valued during the preceding three decades, stretching back to the heyday of DB occupational schemes in the UK.[4] The year 1996 was also prior to the introduction of regulatory changes in the mid-2000s that gave rise to pressure on schemes to 'de-risk' their assets out of 'return-seeking' equities and into 'liability-matching' bonds, to which many attribute the subsequent decline of this form of pension provision. The method employed to value the scheme in the mid-1990s was also roughly along the lines that funded public sector and private multi-employer DB pension schemes are valued in the USA to this day.

In key respects, this is the method of valuation to which the union now representing the interests of scheme members, and their actuarial advisor, would like USS to return, at least insofar as current regulations will permit. They have argued that, by returning to what they regard as sound actuarial and investment practices of the past, the case can be made for funding a generous DB promise at a contribution rate far lower than what both the regulator and the trustee that administers the scheme have recently called for. Should occupational pension schemes return to these practices of valuation and funding, thereby reversing the recent years of decline and atrophy of DB? In this chapter, I shall make the case for such a return and revival, which builds on the arguments advanced in the previous chapter for the pooling of longevity and investment risk within and across generations.

---

[4] In the late 1960s, enrolment in private DB occupational pension schemes in the UK reached its peak when measured by absolute number of members. Such membership has been on the decline ever since, at an especially steep rate since 2008. See Baker and Adams, 'Approaching the Endgame', p. 6.

As of 1996, the assets in the USS pension fund were valued at 108% of the liabilities that had been accrued to date. This valuation of the assets as greater than the liabilities implied that the scheme was in surplus.[5] It was also projected that the scheme would be able to continue to make the same 1/80th final salary DB pension promise in each future year, at the relatively modest and affordable cost of about 20% of salaries, 14% of which would be covered by employers and 6% by members. Were these reasonable and prudent assumptions, grounded in sound methods of valuing a scheme? If they were, why did USS maintain that as of 2020 an overall contribution rate of at least 40% of salaries would be required to provide a less generous pension promise?[6]

The level of funding of pensions that were promised during the previous years of workers' careers, and the required rate of contribution for the making of new pension promises in future years of work leading up to retirement, rest on a set of actuarial assumptions regarding how things will turn out several decades into the future. The scheme's actuary needed to predict what people's final salaries would be, how long they would live in retirement, and what the future rate of price inflation would be. With these assumptions, plus others regarding the composition of the scheme membership, the actuary projected the streams of cash flows that would be paid out of the fund as pensions to retired workers decades into the future. To convert the sum of all these future streams of cash flows into a single figure that captured their present value, the actuary discounted this sum by the expected rate of return on the assets in the scheme. This is the so-called discount rate, which is by far the main source of controversy regarding the proper valuation of a pension scheme. The higher the expected rate of return on the assets in future

---

[5] In 1996 and in prior valuations, the scheme's assets were valued on an 'actuarial' basis rather than being marked to market prices on date of valuation. For all subsequent valuations, USS has valued the assets at market prices. Had USS adopted a market valuation of the assets in 1996, the scheme would have been in greater surplus: 113% rather than 108% funded. (See USS, 'Report by the Actuary on the Actuarial Valuation as at 31 March 1996'.)

[6] By 2020 the 1/80th final salary promise had been reduced to 1/75th of inflation-revalued career average salary for every year of contributing service. (See Joint Expert Panel, 'Report of the Joint Expert Panel', p. 80.) If one factors out the improvement in accrual from 1/80th to 1/75th, the move from a pension based on final salary to one based on career average salary gave rise to an estimated average cut in pension income of roughly 25%. (See First Actuarial, 'Report to the USS Paper', p. 14.)

years, the lower the level of assets and contributions now needed to fully fund the promised pensions.

In valuing the liabilities of the scheme in 1996, the discount rate was assumed to be 8.5% per year. This was an estimate of the annual return on investment of the scheme's assets that would be achieved on average over the next several decades. Although it might now strike many as high, this assumption was in line with prevailing actuarial practices at the time.[7] It was also assumed that retail price index (RPI) inflation would average 5% per annum over the long term. Since, for a scheme such as USS, the liabilities rose and fell with inflation, what was most relevant was the 3.5 percentage point margin between the investment return assumption and the inflation assumption.

How sound was USS's assumption that its assets would grow by around 3.5% each year, in real, RPI-inflation-adjusted terms? To answer this question, we can draw on twenty-six years of actual returns on various types of assets since 1996. On the basis of USS's modelling of the historical portfolio, it appears that the scheme would, in fact, have exceeded the assumed annualized real returns of 3.5% over the next quarter of a century if it had remained invested as it was back then.[8]

Why, then, was the scheme perceived to be in such financial difficulty in 2020? It mainly came down to a discount rate which assumed that returns on the assets in the scheme would *shrink* by 0.5% against RPI each year, for the next thirty years, rather than growing by RPI + 3.5%. It was largely owing to such a pessimistic assumption that USS maintained

---

[7] In 1996, USS's portfolio was invested 75% in equities and 10% in government bonds. (See USS, 'Report by the Actuary on the Actuarial Valuation as at 31 March 1996', Appendix C.) Hence, an 8.5% return assumption was in line with guidance issued by the actuarial profession in 1997, which called for long-term financial assumptions of 9–10% on equities and 8% on government bonds. (See Faculty and Institute of Actuaries, 'GN 27', p. 11.)

[8] See Galvin, 'USS Update', slide 8, for USS's modelling of returns from July 2009 to July 2019 on the historical portfolio in which USS was invested in 2009, which was similar to the portfolio in which USS was invested in previous years, going back to at least 1996. By my calculations involving an updating of these returns, the annualized rate of return on the historical portfolio from the 31 March 1996 to the 31 March 2020 valuation would have been roughly 6.5%, implying about a 3.7% real return above the actual RPI rate of inflation during that period. On account of a dramatic recovery in asset values from the Covid crash of March 2020, the annualized rate of return on the historical portfolio from 31 March 1996 to 31 March 2022 would have been roughly 7.5%, implying about a 4.5% real return.

in 2020 that contributions would need to rise to about 40% of salary to fund what was a less generous pension than what was on offer in 1996.

There are three main reasons why the discount rate in 2020 was lower than the 3.5% over RPI that was assumed in 1996.

First, expected real long-term returns on investments were lower in 2020 than they were in 1996. On USS's best estimates of expected returns in 2020 on different types of assets, the mixture of equities, property, and bonds in which the scheme was invested in the late 1990s was expected to grow by slightly less than 3.0% per annum above RPI between 2020 and 2050.[9] USS's recent best estimates of real returns on equities, property, and bonds in 2020 were therefore not much less optimistic than its historical best estimates of real returns on these same assets when they were held in the late 1990s. This in spite of the fact that the estimates that informed the 2020, but not the 1996, valuation were made in the light of experience of the bursting of the dotcom bubble in the early 2000s and the long aftermath of the global financial crisis of 2007–08.

The second and much more significant reason for the lower discount rate was that the portfolio out of which USS planned to fund its DB promises in 2020 was much more heavily weighted towards bonds than the historical portfolio. Like many DB portfolios back then, USS's was about 80% invested in equities in the years leading up to the global financial crisis. The remaining 20% was split between property and government bonds. After the global financial crisis, USS embarked upon a rebalancing of its portfolio away from equities and property. This shift was of a piece with a more general trend to 'de-risk' assets held by DB schemes. In 2006, 61% of assets in private sector DB schemes in the UK were invested in equities and only 28% in bonds. In 2020, these proportions were more than completely reversed, with 69% investment

---

[9] In its 'Consultation for the 2020 Valuation', USS assumed that real (RPI) return on equities would be about 3.7% per annum over the next thirty years, for property about 1.1% per annum, and for nominal thirty-year government bonds about –1.8% per annum (see table 8.1). USS expressed real returns in relation to the consumer price index (CPI). But it also assumed that RPI would exceed CPI by about 0.7%. Since CPI was introduced in the UK only in 2003, and the 1996 valuation employs RPI whose history extends from 1947 to the present, I have translated more recent CPI figures into RPI to allow for like-for-like comparison of inflation-indexed figures in recent and older valuations.

in bonds and only 20% in equities.[10] The portfolio into which USS plans to invest over the next several decades, in order to fund pension promises made up to the year 2020, will average out to roughly one third so-called 'growth assets' which encompass equities and property and the other two thirds in bonds and other so-called 'liability-matching assets'. This shift away from growth assets has significantly reduced the expected return on the portfolio down from the aforementioned nearly 3% above RPI to about 1.25% above RPI.[11]

The returns I have just quoted are those that one can expect on average per annum over the long run. Back in the 1990s, the discount rate was set on the basis of such expected returns on the assets. According, however, to currently prevailing regulations, 'economic and actuarial assumptions must be chosen prudently, taking account...of an appropriate margin for adverse deviation'.[12] On USS's application of this requirement, the discount rate for the 2020 valuation was set on the basis of returns that one could expect to achieve about 75–80% of the time rather than merely on average.[13] This is the third reason why the discount rate for the 2020 valuation was so much lower than it was in 1996. The application of such prudence lowered the discount rate from 1.25% above RPI to about 0.5% *below* RPI.

When pension contributions are set on the assumption that long-term returns on the assets into which they will be invested will fall half a percentage point short of RPI, as opposed to the assumption that prevailed during the 1990s that returns will exceed RPI by 3.5%, it shouldn't come as a surprise that members and employers were called on to pay much more for a less good DB pension in 2020.

---

[10] See Pension Protection Fund, *The Purple Book*, p. 2.

[11] The reduction is so significant on account of the fact that USS expected UK government bonds to underperform equities by about 5.5–6 percentage points per annum, and corporate bonds to underperform equities by about 2.75 percentage points, between 2020 and 2050. (See USS, 'Consultation for the 2020 Valuation', table 8.1.)

[12] UK Parliament, 'Occupational Pension Schemes Regulations', regulation 5(4)(a).

[13] For a portfolio weighted towards growth assets, the geometric mean return will be greater than the median 50th percentile return, given a positive skew in the distribution towards high returns. Stochastic analysis that USS performed in 2018 on its 'reference portfolio', which was then about 65% invested in growth assets, revealed a median nominal return of 5.3% but a geometric mean return of 6.0%. (See USS, 'A Technical Overview of the 2017 Valuation', at 33 min. 30 sec. of the video.)

Was there sound justification for requiring members and their employers to pay so much more for a less good pension? That is the question to which I shall now turn.

The answer to this question turns crucially on the answer to the following question: What is the appropriate rate at which to discount the pension payments promised many years in the future, in order to convert those future cash flows into a single present value? According to UK regulations, the discount rate

must be chosen prudently, taking into account either or both—

(i) the yield on assets held by the scheme to fund future benefits and the anticipated future investment returns, and

(ii) the market redemption yields on government or other high-quality bonds[14]

In its 1996 valuation, USS followed the first of the two approaches enumerated above, save for one crucial aspect: back then, there was no requirement that the discount rate be chosen prudently. Accordingly, USS discounted on the basis of its best estimates of the 'long term average rates of return' on the various assets in the scheme, with no downward pessimistic adjustment in the name of prudence.[15] In so doing, USS was following standard actuarial practices of the time for setting the discount rate.

These two approaches track a stark divide between two different schools of thought regarding the valuation and funding of a DB pension, the former arising from the traditional practices of actuaries and the latter arising from more recent theories from financial economics. In what follows, I shall defend the actuarial approach as properly grounded in the conception of a pension scheme which emerged from the previous chapter as an ongoing corporate entity which remains evergreen, through the influx of new members to replace those who retire, thereby

---

[14] UK Parliament, 'Occupational Pension Schemes Regulations', regulation 5(4)(b)(i)–(ii).
[15] USS, 'Report by the Actuary on the Actuarial Valuation as at 31 March 1996', 7.1.2. As this is spelled out in the previous valuation, 'on average the "good" years are expected to be better than the "bad" years to the extent shown in the assumptions' (USS, 'Report by the Actuary on the Actuarial Valuation as at 31 March 1993', p. 11).

making it possible to pool investment risks indefinitely across as well as within generations. To defend the actuarial approach, I must also explain why the second, mutually incompatible bond-based approach to the setting of the discount rate is unsound. I shall turn first to this critical task. In addition to exposing fundamental flaws in a highly influential approach to pension valuation, my critique of the financial economics approach will clear the ground for the more positive defence of the actuarial approach which I shall go on to develop.

On the bond-based approach to the setting of the discount rate, which is grounded in a theory of value from financial economics, the possibility of pooling the investment risk of the scheme's growth assets across generations is irrelevant to its valuation and funding. This is because, according to this theory, the discounting of pension liabilities has nothing to do with the return on the assets held in a scheme's fund. Rather, irrespective of whether these assets are *actually* held by the scheme, the sound measure of the value of the liabilities is the return on those financial assets that 'match the liabilities' by providing streams of cash flows that are equivalent to those of a promised pension, in their magnitude and duration and the level of certainty that they will be delivered.[16]

The theory behind such a discount rate is as follows. Irrespective of how the pension fund is invested, such financial assets provide an accurate measure of the value of the liabilities (i.e., the promised pension payments) in the following respect: assuming that such a trade is possible, one party should be willing to exchange the promised pension payments for a portfolio of financial assets which are guaranteed, to as high a degree, to produce the promised cash flows. These will be bonds of the right temporal duration and level of inflation protection, which also reflect the credit risk of the employer's not coming through with the pension payments.[17] If individuals were allowed to trade their pension

---

[16] 'Financial economists generally argue that defined benefit pension liabilities should be valued by discounting future benefit payments using a yield rate for a bond with comparable duration and risk as the liabilities' (Turner et al., 'Determining Discount Rates', p. 4).

[17] Long-dated, inflation-indexed government bonds are securities which perhaps most closely match the magnitude and duration of a typical DB pension promise. Since they are backed by the government, they will, however, generally reflect a lower credit risk than the risk that sponsoring private employers will default on their pension obligations. For this reason (among others—see also n. 18), their yield will be lower than that of a truly matching asset.

promises, they might be willing to exchange them for other financial assets, such as equities, or a lump sum of money they can spend now rather than when they retire. But given how closely the bond portfolio I have just described matches the various characteristics of a pension, they should be willing to trade their pensions for such bonds, irrespective of their particular preferences for money in retirement, or risk. Given this willingness to exchange their promised pension payments for this portfolio of bonds, the market value of the latter accurately reflects the exchange value of these pensions for most workers.[18]

Here are two related reasons why the lower expected return on bonds, rather than higher expected return on growth assets such as equities and property, provides a discount rate that accurately measures the market exchange value of the pension promise. First, one can expect the DB pension one's employer has promised to be delivered with a fairly high level of certainty. Hence one would expose oneself to a fair amount of downside risk of lower-than-expected income in retirement if one traded one's pension promise for a portfolio of growth assets whose returns are expected merely on average to equal one's pension payments. Second, even if one is not risk averse, it is rational for the following reason to refuse a growth portfolio of equities and property whose higher returns are expected to equal the promised pensions: that growth portfolio will have a lower market value than a liability-matching bond portfolio whose lower returns are also expected to equal one's promised pensions. Hence, one would be able to sell the liability-matching portfolio to purchase a more valuable growth portfolio than the one which is expected on average to match the liabilities.[19]

---

[18] It is, in fact, illegal for an individual to sell one's occupational pension in the UK, whereas government bonds are publicly tradeable assets. Their 'liquidity price premium', relative to pension promises, provides a respect in which the yield on government bonds will be lower than that of assets that truly match a pension promise. (See Novy-Marx and Rauh, 'The Liabilities and Risks of State-Sponsored Pension Plans', p. 196.) It is, however, possible for a pension scheme to transfer its obligations to meet its pension promises by means of an insurance company buy-out. The cost of such a transaction tracks the value of a portfolio of government and/or high-quality corporate bonds with cash flows that approximate those of the pension promises.

[19] See American Academy of Actuaries, 'Measuring Pension Obligations', pp. 2–3, including n. 3.

The financial economists' approach is appropriate for the valuation of a pension promise, understood as the price it makes sense to pay to buy or sell this promise.[20] Such a valuation is akin to such familiar valuations as that of a house, where what is being ascertained is how much money that property would exchange for if placed on the market.

It can be shown, however, that a so-called actuarial valuation of pension liabilities is very different from a determination of the market exchange value of those liabilities.[21] An actuarial valuation does not actually involve a valuation of the liabilities. Rather, its purpose is to determine whether the pension contributions into the scheme to date have been invested in a manner that is 'sufficient and appropriate' to 'make provision for the scheme's liabilities'.[22] This purpose is captured by a term known as the 'technical provisions', which is a requirement of an insurer or pension scheme to hold assets sufficient to ensure that it can meet its liabilities. As is stated by the 'statutory funding objective' of the UK Pensions Act 2004:

(1) Every scheme is subject to a requirement ("the statutory funding objective") that it must have sufficient and appropriate assets to cover its technical provisions.

(2) A scheme's "technical provisions" means the amount required, on an actuarial calculation, to make provision for the scheme's liabilities.[23]

---

[20] As Turner et al. explain:

This approach arguably is the correct way to value pension liabilities when determining...the price at which the liabilities could be transferred to another party. The financial economists' approach is the approach to be used by someone considering buying the liability—the greater the risk [of failure to deliver the pension that has been promised], the lower the price the person is willing to pay (the higher the discount rate) [to purchase that pension promise].

('Determining Discount Rates', p. 4)

[21] As John Kay said about forty years ago:

much of the disagreement between [actuaries and financial economists] rests on what is a semantic confusion. The source of this semantic confusion, I believe, is that it is the practice of actuaries to describe an exercise of determining appropriate contribution rates for a pension funding as a "valuation"...but it is not a valuation as the man in the street or I, as an economist, understand the word valuation.

(As quoted in E. A. Johnston, 'The Comparative Value of Pensions', p. 22)

[22] In addition to determining whether adequate provision has been made for such past promises, the valuation also serves the purpose of setting the level of the contributions that will be required in subsequent years to make and later fulfil new pension promises (future promises).

[23] UK Parliament, 'Pensions Act 2004', sec. 222(1)–(2).

The amount required to provide for the liabilities is not necessarily the value—market or otherwise—of the liabilities.

One's 'liabilities' are simply the total amount that one has promised to pay in pensions, far into the future. This amount is calculated in the manner I described earlier. The undiscounted sum total of these future cash flows will typically be far greater than the market value of the assets in a pension scheme. The question then arises as to how to appropriately discount these future cash flows, to convert them into a sum of money today: a so-called present value. A discount rate provides an accurate monetization of the value of workers' promised pensions when it matches the rate of return on a portfolio of assets for which they would now be willing to exchange their promises. But a discount rate which is 'sufficient and appropriate' to 'make provision for the scheme's liabilities' need not be as low as the rate of return on the liability-matching assets of a portfolio with which workers would be willing to exchange their pension promises. Financial economists are therefore mistaken in claiming that a market valuation should be employed to determine whether a pension scheme is fully funded, where the latter is the purpose of an actuarial valuation.[24]

I shall offer two arguments for why the yield of a bond portfolio that matches the liabilities does not necessarily provide the discount rate for the 'technical provisions'.

My first argument begins with the observation that existing, and sound, regulatory practices typically require that a weaker, less creditworthy sponsoring employer put in more contributions to make provision for a given pension promise than a stronger, more creditworthy sponsor.[25] The rationale for this is that one can allow the more creditworthy

---

[24] For evidence that they make this claim, see Turner et al., 'Determining Discount Rates', p. 4; Brown and Pennacchi, 'Discounting Pension Liabilities', pp. 254–5 and 258; and Exley, Mehta, and Smith, 'The Financial Theory of Defined Benefit Pension Schemes'. Turner et al. capture the manner in which this claim is mistaken when they write that the 'determination of the discount rate' for the purpose of 'calculating required contributions for funding liabilities for an ongoing defined benefit plan' is 'a regulatory issue rather than purely a financial markets issue. Regulators use that rate to assure a certain degree the security of the pension promises made to workers, rather than to value liabilities for the purpose of buying or selling them' ('Determining Discount Rates', p. 4).

[25] I say 'typically' because this requirement of a greater contribution might be attenuated if the sponsoring employer is so weak that this would threaten their solvency or sustainability.

employer—whose 'covenant' will be stronger, for that reason—to put in less by way of contributions now because they are more able to put in more contributions later if returns on the assets into which these contributions have been invested turn out lower than expected.[26] A less creditworthy sponsor's pension promise will, however, be worth *less* to a worker than a more creditworthy sponsor's promise of the same pension payments, for the simple reason that the worker is rightly less certain that she will end up receiving the full amount of the pension she has been promised. Hence, when one values a pension promise as the bond portfolio with which one would be willing to trade it, one will insist on more expensive bonds with a higher credit rating—e.g., AAA rather than AA—in order to part with a pension that a highly creditworthy employer has promised, as compared with one that a less creditworthy employer has promised. A DB pension that Trinity College Cambridge promises will be worth more than a pension promise from a scheme whose sole sponsor is on the edge of insolvency. It does not follow, however, that Trinity College should be required to put more money into its pension fund than the employer on the brink of insolvency, in order to make sufficient provision for its pensions. Given the primary objective of pension regulations to ensure that the benefits promised to members are paid, the very opposite is true.[27] Yet setting the technical provisions as the market exchange value of a pension promise would have the perverse consequence of requiring Trinity College to put in more money to secure its pension promises than an employer on the edge of insolvency.[28]

---

[26] As the Pensions Regulator's code states: 'the higher the level of investment risk held within the scheme the greater should be the trustees' focus on the level of employer covenant available to support it' ('Code of Practice No. 3', sec. 98). The regulator defines the 'employer covenant' as 'the extent of the employer's legal obligation and financial ability to support the scheme now and in the future' ('Ten Key Points', point 1).

[27] Among the main objectives of the regulator are 'to protect the benefits under occupational pension schemes, of, or in respect of, members of such schemes' and 'to reduce the risk of situations arising which may lead to compensation being payable from the Pension Protection Fund' (UK Parliament, 'Pensions Act 2004', secs. 5(1)(a) and 5(1)(c)). Both objectives tell in favour of less, rather than more, creditworthy sponsors being required to put in higher contributions to back a given pension promise.

[28] Although they endorse the financial economics approach to setting the discount rate, Novy-Marx and Rauh implicitly recognize this problem, when they write that

using taxable state municipal bond discount rates, as opposed to the risk-free Treasury rate, essentially credits states for the possibility that they can default on pension liabilities. Thus, it would be highly misleading to use a liability measure

I now turn to my second argument for why the yield of a bond portfolio that matches the liabilities does not necessarily provide the discount rate for the technical provisions. The technical provisions are 'the amount required' to 'make provision for' pension promises by funding them in advance rather than as and when the promised payments arise. They are therefore essentially a collateral requirement.[29] As my earlier discussion has revealed, it follows from the nature of a pension promise that bonds will provide a closer match to, and a better substitute for, a pension than other financial assets such as equities. As I shall now demonstrate, it is, however, a fallacy to maintain that the bond-like nature of a pension liability gives rise to a requirement to fund it out of matching bonds, or, if not that, at least to a level sufficient to purchase such bonds.

Regulated DB pensions are essentially non-tradeable bonds, issued to workers by a trustee rather than their employer, in exchange for contributions. As we have seen, these regulations involve a collateral requirement. A corporation may, however, issue unsecured bonds to its own employees, which replicate nearly all the characteristics of a DB pension. The promised cash flows might, for example, be linked to inflation, in the manner of a pension. In 2018, Cambridge University issued long-dated bonds whose payments were inflation-linked. A corporation may issue a bond whose duration is at least as long as that of the longest pension liability. In 2017, Oxford University issued bonds of 100-year duration, which is longer than all but the most unusual DB pension liabilities involving very young surviving spouses or other eligible dependants.[30]

arising from this method as a benchmark for pension funding. A state with poor credit quality should not set aside less money to fund its pensions simply because it has a high probability of defaulting on its obligations.
('The Liabilities and Risks of State-Sponsored Pension Plans', p. 197)

Brown and Pennacchi offer a related objection to the use of a discount rate that reflects the market value of the pension promise to determine how well funded the pension scheme is. Their argument appeals to the fact that the market value approach might generate the absurd consequence that 'the pension plan becomes fully funded as the value of assets shrinks'. This is for the reason that if a decrease in the value of the assets held by the scheme 'drives the probability of the plan sponsor making good on its promises toward zero, then the market value of the liability can disappear completely' ('Discounting Pension Liabilities', pp. 260–1).

[29] As the Pensions Regulator's funding code states: 'An important purpose of scheme assets is to provide collateral and security for the promised benefits' ('Code of Practice No. 3', sec. 88).

[30] There is one case of entitlement to a veteran's pension that was accrued by a US soldier in the American Civil War in 1864 and 1865, in which the pension liability was fully discharged

A corporation may also issue a perpetual, whereby it pledges to provide an income stream forever. Since a perpetual has no maturity date, there is no date by which the issuer pledges to return the principal. Alternatively, a corporate bond may take the form of an amortizing bond, with final principal to be returned on date of maturity. The payments of a corporate bond might begin only when the bondholder has reached a specified retirement age. The bond could also be set to mature at the date, as determined by mortality tables, when one expects someone of the bondholder's age to die.

More generally, the ubiquity of corporate bonds which are unsecured—i.e., which are not backed by collateral—shows that the mere fact that a DB pension involves a bond-like promise does not imply that it must be funded to a level sufficient to allow for the purchase of bonds that match the pension liabilities. For, if it did imply this, then, by parity of reasoning, one would need to insist that a corporation may not issue a bond unless it secures it with assets that match the liability. It would, however, defeat the point of issuing corporate bonds if one were required to secure them in this manner from the outset. One would hardly be able to issue bonds to raise much cash to invest in anything other than the securing of those very bonds. Rather, one would have to use up the money from bond sales to purchase comparable bonds to serve as their collateral.

It is, therefore, a mistake for financial economists to maintain that the bond-like nature of a pension promise gives rise to a requirement that it be secured by means of funding to the level of the value of a liability-matching bond. This mistake is puzzling, given that such financial economists do not also claim that the even more bond-like nature of a corporate bond has the implication, which I have just shown to be nonsensical, that one may not issue such a bond unless it is secured by fully matching assets.

The pension-like corporate bond I described above falls short, in one significant respect, of a genuine pension promise. Recall that the date of maturity of this bond was linked not to the actual date of death of the

---

only upon the death in 2020 of a daughter who had been eligible to inherit the pension as a dependant on account of her cognitive disability. See Lilleston, 'Last American to Collect a Civil War Pension'.

bondholder but rather to the expected date of death of someone of that person's age, as determined by mortality tables. If the date of maturity of a bond that pays a regular fixed income is linked to the actual date of death of the bondholder, it becomes an annuity, which only a highly regulated insurance company may sell to the general public. These regulations call for the backing of an annuity by assets which guarantee, to a very high probability, that the company will be able to pay what has been promised. To provide such a guarantee, it will invest in liability-matching assets largely comprising of bonds. As I have just shown, it is not, however, the bond-like nature of an annuity which mandates such backing.

What is the justification for imposing demanding collateral require-ments on both annuities and pensions, which are bonds identical in nature to the unsecured corporate bond I sketched above, except that the date of maturity is set to the bondholder's actual, rather than expected, date of death? The answer is that it is in the public interest, as a matter of consumer protection, to regulate the private contracts and arrangements that give rise to both annuities and pensions. While 'let the buyer beware' might be appropriate when applied to the large institutions or wealthy individuals who might trade in corporate bonds, it is not appropriate in the case of the typical individual who is trying to ensure that sufficient provision has been made for his or her retirement. The regulation of pensions and annuities has been shaped by stories of ordinary individ-uals who have been hard done by the providers of financial security in their retirement. We lack similar tales of ordinary individuals who have suffered on account of their direct transactions with unscrupulous sellers of corporate bonds.[31] The private individual stands in more need of protection against loss than the institutional trader.

To provide further evidence that it is considerations of consumer protection, rather than the bond-like nature of a pension liability, which provides the rationale for the regulatory requirement to fund a DB pension up to a high level, I note that there is nothing in law in either

---

[31] The global financial crisis gave rise to calls for the greater regulation of securities. But this was at least in part on account of the devastation wrought in a more indirect manner on ordinary individuals by that crisis.

the UK or the USA to stop a private employer from setting up an unfunded pension scheme for one of their own employees with payments extending from retirement to death. Unlike the corporate bond in my earlier example, here the bond takes the form of an annuity whose maturity is pegged to the death of the holder. The catch is that such an unfunded DB pension scheme would not be authorized as eligible for the favourable tax treatment that funded pension schemes enjoy. The bond-like nature of what is promised here is no different from that of a funded pension, apart from the fact that the promise is not backed by any collateral security. If a requirement to fund to the level of matching bonds is justified in the case of an authorized DB pension scheme, but not an unauthorized one, this must be on account of public policy considerations rather than implied by a theory of the economic value of bonds. These unfunded pensions are, in fact, offered only to employees who are so highly paid that their pension is largely ineligible for favourable tax treatment.[32] These individuals are not in need of the level of consumer protection and security of retirement benefits of workers on more average pay. It is, moreover, a matter of sound public policy considerations, rather than a truth of financial economics, that favourable tax treatment is not extended to the most highly paid workers.

I have shown that financial economics does not provide a justification for a requirement that a tax-sheltered pension promise be secured by contributions ringfenced in a fund guarded by a trustee, whose value is so high that it is possible to purchase a bond portfolio that comes close to matching the DB liability. Is there, however, a *regulatory* justification, grounded in sound public policy considerations, for such a demanding requirement? It is to this question that I now turn. I shall begin by presenting what I take to be the best justification of this latter type for the relevance of the yield on a liability-matching bond portfolio to the setting of the discount rate for the purpose of determining whether the assets held by a scheme are sufficient to provide for the pensions that have been promised.

---

[32] In the UK, for example, tax relief is provided, within annual and lifetime limits exceeded by highly paid employees, on DC contributions into the pension scheme and capital gains on returns on the investment of those contributions, and on the increase in, and overall, value of accrual of entitlement to DB pensions.

A growth portfolio will have a higher expected return than an equally priced government bond portfolio whose promised rate of return is regarded as risk-free. This higher payoff has been described as an 'equity risk premium', which is the compensation regarded as necessary to induce someone to spend a given amount of money on equities rather than bonds, on account of the greater risk, to which people are averse, of holding the former.[33] The stronger a sponsoring employer, the greater their ability to put more assets into the pension fund in the event that returns on these riskier growth assets are less good than expected. For this reason, the stronger the sponsor, the higher the assumed rate of return on the assets by which the regulator will allow them to discount the liabilities.

A relatively weak sponsor who is less able to demonstrate the ability to make good large funding shortfalls will be required to invest more expensively at the outset in financial assets that run a lesser risk of falling short of covering pension promises. A sponsor who is so weak that they are able to demonstrate hardly any ability to make good a future shortfall will be required to almost entirely pre-fund their pension promises. They must invest at the outset in a portfolio of financial assets such as long-dated, inflation-linked government and high-quality corporate bonds that come close to matching their pension liabilities in duration and magnitude. Such a portfolio will approximate the composition of a portfolio that backs a genuinely matching asset for a pension liability: an insurance company annuity. Hence a very weak sponsor will be required to discount their pension liabilities at something close to the risk-free government bond yield.

By contrast, a strong sponsor will be permitted, at less expense, to discount their liabilities at a higher rate of expected return of investment in growth assets which are deemed sufficiently likely to cover the promised pension payments in future years. They will be allowed to do this, so long as they can demonstrate an ability to underwrite the investment risk by showing how they will deliver their pension promises in the event that

---

[33] According to a statement from the Pensions Regulator in March 2020: 'We note from a range of long-term forecasts provided by investment managers and advisers that the risk premium of growth vs matching assets (best estimate) is in the range of 3–5% pa' ('Defined Benefit Funding Code of Practice', p. 95, para. 399).

returns on their growth assets are less good than expected. How might they demonstrate this? One way is by showing that, in the event that the downside risks of growth assets materialize, they will have the where-withal to purchase a liability-matching bond portfolio that has a very high chance of covering all the promised pension payments. It is for this reason, among others, that the regulator pays close attention to the extent to which the assumed rate of return on the assets held by the scheme—which is to say the discount rate—exceeds the risk-free rate. The sponsor will be called upon to demonstrate the following: that they have the resources to make good the gap between the lower price of a growth portfolio with higher expected returns, and the higher price of a bond portfolio with lower expected returns, even in the event that this gap grows larger on account of either a fall in the stock market or a decline in the yields of bonds. In the useful metaphor USS's chief risk officer, the 'safe harbour' of a liability-matching bond portfolio must remain within affordable reach.[34]

Fig. 2.1 provides a key to understanding the difficulties in which DB pension schemes which are regulated in this manner have found them-selves in recent years. In the mid-1990s, the risk-free rate of long-dated government bonds that matched pension liabilities was so high that, even though the scheme was heavily invested in equities and assuming an 8.5% rate of return on its assets, USS nevertheless had more than enough assets in the fund to cover the purchase of a liability-matching bond portfolio. USS was 125% funded on a solvency basis in 1996, which was pegged to the cost of purchasing 'a mixture of index-linked and fixed interest sterling securities' that replicated the portfolio of an insurance company annuity.[35] Although it remained in surplus on a solvency basis for the next two valuations, by 2005 USS was underfunded on this basis, on account of falls in both the stock market and government bond yields. As bond yields continued to fall, reaching historic lows in more recent years, the safe harbour of a liability-matching bond portfolio became prohibitively expensive. USS was only about 50% funded on a solvency basis in 2020, which is to say that the assets held in the scheme at date of

---

[34] See USS, 'Methodology and Risk Appetite for the 2020 Valuation', p. 26.
[35] USS, 'Report by the Actuary on the Actuarial Valuation as at 31 March 1996', p. 17.

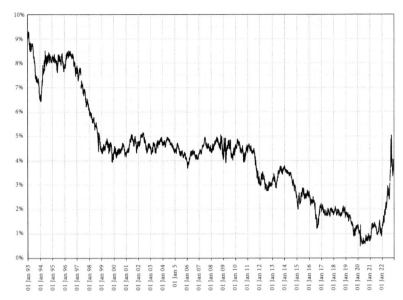

Fig. 2.1 Nominal yield of twenty-year UK government bonds (gilts)
Source: Bank of England Database. https://www.bankofengland.co.uk/boeapps/database/
© Bank of England under terms of Open Government Licence. https://www.nationalarchives.
gov.uk/doc/open-government-licence/version/3/

valuation were worth only about 50% of the cost of the purchase of a liability-matching bond portfolio. Employers would have to have come up with an extra £63 billion to purchase such a portfolio.[36] Such a sum was far beyond what they could afford to raise in the short term.

At the time of the 2020 valuation, USS's trustee called for a safe harbour to be within affordable reach in the following respect: that it be possible for employers to raise sufficient cash by means of further contributions of not more than 10% of payroll per annum over the next three decades, in order to enhance the market value of the assets in the portfolio to a level which would make it possible to purchase a liability-matching bond portfolio.[37] The time period of three decades was chosen because it had been deemed that the higher education sector would be in sufficiently strong financial condition to pay this level of further

---

[36]   USS, 'Actuarial Valuation Report at 31 March 2020', p. 9.
[37]   These 10% contributions would be in addition to employer contributions of 15% of payroll per annum to provide for the future pension accrual of members.

contributions for at least that many years. Bond yields were so low at the date of the valuation, however, and hence a liability-matching portfolio so expensive, that USS would have fallen short of being able to purchase such a portfolio at those low yields even with thirty years of further contributions of 10% of payroll per annum.[38]

Does a DB scheme need to be within such affordable reach of a liability-matching bond portfolio? Or might it prudently fund pension promises out of a portfolio of growth assets whose value falls so far short of that of a liability-matching portfolio that one could not afford to purchase such a portfolio, even after three decades of significant extra pension contributions? In what follows, I shall make the case that such a safe harbour is unnecessary for an open, ongoing scheme such as USS. I shall also argue that USS provides a model for how DB schemes throughout the private sector can and should manage investment risk in the absence of such a safe harbour.

In 2020 it was estimated that returns as modest as RPI + 0.5% were all that was needed to fully fund the USS DB pension promise out of contributions of as little as 26% of payroll.[39] This was comfortably 2% below the best estimate of returns on the portfolio in which the scheme was invested at the time, which was about 65% weighted towards growth assets. With such a prudent margin by which the returns on the assets might fall short of a best estimate, while still covering the costs of all promised pensions, the risks of remaining largely invested in growth assets were low for an open, ongoing scheme such as USS.

The positive cash flow of such a scheme over a long investment time horizon served to mitigate these risks. A pension scheme's cash flow is its annual income minus its annual expenses. It is positive when its income exceeds its expenses. The primary sources of income are employer and

---

[38] See USS, 'Monitoring of the 2020 Financial Management Plan', p. 4. Here I am simplifying some of the details of the actual risk metric that USS employed. This metric was more demanding insofar as it also involved the building in of a further margin of safety to account for 'the risk of deterioration in the funding level during the process of de-risking the investments as part of moving to' a liability-matching portfolio (USS, 'A Consultation for the 2020 Valuation', p. 67). It was, however, less demanding insofar as the 'safe harbour' involved a 'self-sufficiency' portfolio which was less expensive than, and did not match the assets as closely as, the replicated annuity portfolio of a solvency valuation.

[39] See UUK, 'UUK Representatives' Views', p. 2.

worker pension contributions and investment income from the assets in the pension fund (e.g., stock dividends, bond coupon payments). The primary expense is the payment of promised pensions to those in retirement. When a scheme remains open to the new membership of the workers who are employed to replace those who have retired on at least a one-for-one basis, a sufficiently large and stable proportion of workers to pensioners over time will ensure that the annual cash inflow of contributions combined with investment income will always exceed the annual payment of pensions to those in retirement. In the case of USS, projections have indicated that incoming contributions plus a modest level of investment income from growth assets would be sufficient to meet all pension promises in any given year, for at least the next fifty years.[40]

A positive cash flow is not in itself sufficient to establish full funding.[41] Nevertheless, it serves to establish the prudence of a less expensive funding of a scheme out of the higher expected returns of growth assets. It does so by mitigating the risk of remaining invested for the long term in equities and property, rather than ever needing to embark on the more expensive journey to the safe harbour of a liability-matching bond portfolio. The mitigation takes the form of the elimination of the disinvestment risk of being forced to sell growth assets at an inopportune time.[42] Rather, it provides a scheme with the liberty to sell such assets as and when market conditions appear favourable. A positive cash flow also

---

[40] See Salt and Benstead, 'Progressing the Valuation', pp. 10–14.

[41] A scheme will be underfunded just in case the investment returns on contributions are insufficient to cover the cost of the pension promises associated with these contributions. Such underfunding is, however, consistent with a scheme's being cash flow positive simply on account of increases in contributions arising from the growth of membership, year on year. In such a scenario, it will remain possible to pay pensions as they fall due for as long as the membership is growing. But pensions promised in the past would be paid through the raiding of contributions for future promises. Here the scheme would be well funded because cash flow is positive in something approaching the illusory manner in which a pyramid scheme is well funded because cash flow is positive.

[42] As First Actuarial explains:

> While the net cash flow is positive, there is no need to sell any assets and therefore no disinvestment risk to the USS. [Therefore,] a measure of risk which suggests a market fall is a problem would be giving a wrong message.... While there is no requirement to sell assets, volatility from market value fluctuations is not a concern for the USS. ('Report to the USS Paper', p. 27)

facilitates long-term investment in growth assets such as infrastructure, whose expected returns attract a premium owing to their illiquidity.[43] Moreover, since a scheme that will remain open and cash flow positive indefinitely can hold growth assets in perpetuity, its trustee can be fairly confident that it will be able, over the long term, to reap returns that will be sufficient to cover the cost of the promised pensions, at least so long as assumptions regarding returns on investments are relatively prudent.

Of course, even with a decent margin of prudence, below which the returns on growth assets might fall short of a best estimate while still covering the cost of the promised pensions, there remains a risk that these returns will fall significantly below this margin. Does such downside risk fall within the bounds of acceptability? Stochastic modelling 'shows that higher risk investments tend to perform better over the long term' and 'the probability of loss decreases over time'.[44] With a portfolio weighted towards growth assets, not only will the probability of loss decrease over time. On reasonable assumptions involving returns and variance, the average monetary value of the losses multiplied by the probability of loss will decrease with time once one has held these assets for more than a relatively short number of years.[45] Unfortunately, the following significant downside risk remains: 'the potential size of any loss that occurs *increases*' with time.[46] In particular, the magnitude of the worst possible outcome increases with time.[47]

Moreover, the desire to protect against such downside risk helps to explain why there is such demand for the long-dated bonds issued by governments and other institutions with exceptionally high credit

---

[43] See Silcock, 'DC Scheme Investment in Illiquid and Alternative Assets'. As noted there, the lack of a tight correlation between the value of infrastructure and the price of listed equities provides a form of diversification that further mitigates the risk of holding a growth portfolio.

[44] USS, 'Methodology and Risk Appetite for the 2020 Valuation', p. 22. As Zvi Bodie writes:

> it is indeed true that the probability of a shortfall declines with the length of the investment time horizon. For example, suppose the rate of return on stocks is log-normally distributed with a risk premium of 8 percent per year and an annualized standard deviation of 20 percent. With a time horizon of only one year, the probability of a shortfall is 34 percent, whereas at twenty years that probability is only 4 percent.
>
> ('Mismatch Risk, Government Guarantees, and Financial Instability', p. 278)

[45] Con Keating has shown this in unpublished stochastic modelling.

[46] USS, 'Methodology and Risk Appetite for the 2020 Valuation', p. 22 (my emphasis added).

[47] Bodie, 'Mismatch Risk, Government Guarantees, and Financial Instability', p. 278.

ratings. As Exley, Mehta, and Smith explain, the belief that it is 'highly likely in the long term' that equities will generate sufficient return to cover one's liabilities

> manifestly fails to explain why anyone would be prepared to purchase long dated bonds at their market price, if they can be synthesised for so much less [out of a portfolio of equities]. The key must lie in the unlikely event where the equities fail to be adequate. Although the probability of this event may be small, it bears heavily on the minds of investors as a whole. We can see why—a promise which holds fast when everything else has collapsed all around is potentially very valuable.[48]

A funded DB promise is now regarded as the sort of thing that one is meant to be able to rely upon, even in adverse circumstances in which 'everything else has collapsed all around'. Throughout a global pandemic which gave rise to a record-breaking collapse in gross domestic product, for example, DB pension promises were paid on time and in full by private, funded schemes. But, as Exley, Mehta, and Smith note, if anyone could synthesize equities, at lesser expense, into assets that provide the same cash flows as bonds, come what may, then nobody would ever purchase long-dated bonds. There is, however, clearly high demand for such bonds. To respond to this challenge, one must show that DB pension schemes are in a better position than others to manage the downside risks of growth assets such as equities and property: even though others must purchase bonds because the downside risks of growth assets are too great for them to tolerate, DB schemes have opportunities to manage the risks of such high-return assets that are not widely available.[49]

---

[48] Exley, Mehta, and Smith, 'The Financial Theory of Defined Benefit Pension Schemes', p. 870.

[49] As mentioned above, long-term investment in infrastructure provides an example of such an opportunity. This opportunity will not be widely available, given the scale of such investment, as well as its illiquidity risk. See Silcock, 'DC Scheme Investment in Illiquid and Alternative Assets'.

Here is how a DB pension scheme is able to navigate the open seas of growth assets even if it remains too far from the safe harbour of a liability-matching bond portfolio in which to take refuge: how it can hunker down and ride out the vortex of even a large drop in their value. So long as it is possible to foresee that it will be cash flow positive for the next several decades, there is no need for such a scheme to quickly repair a deficit in funding in order to meet its 'key duty to pay promised benefits as they fall due'.[50] These pensions involve many small and predictable payments that stretch several decades into the future. An open, ongoing, cash flow positive scheme can therefore spread deficit recovery payments over several decades to recover from even very large losses over time.[51]

It is here that the wide and inclusive multi-employer arrangement of a DB pension scheme such as USS plays a crucial role. Even though not every single employer can be counted on to be around and financially strong enough to make deficit recovery payments over several decades, the UK higher education sector as a whole can be relied upon to remain financially solvent over the long run. The so-called last man standing (LMS) mutuality of USS ensures that there will be an enduring corporate body capable of making good on debts whose repayments have been amortized over several decades. If any one employer becomes insolvent, responsibility to make good any underfunding of their promises is automatically shared by the other employers through small increases in their contributions. The LMS federation is therefore a form of insurance in which losses from insolvency are geographically spread out evenly and thinly among the large number of remaining solvent employers across the UK. This is the insurance of a mutual association, which pre-dates

---

[50] The Pensions Regulator, 'Code of Practice No. 3', p. 7.

[51] See Turner et al.:

> We argue that a higher rate than that conceived by financial economists can be used for discounting liabilities for regulatory purposes because an ongoing plan sponsor has the option, and presumably the ability, of making additional future contributions if needed. A counter argument to this approach relates to the timing of when additional contributions would be needed. Additional required contributions [to make up for investment returns turning out less well than expected] would tend to be needed when the stock market, and presumably the plan sponsor, were doing poorly, which is a bad time to need to make additional contributions. This argument is considerably weakened when it is recognized that regulators generally allow plans to amortize losses over a number of years. ('Determining Discount Rates', p. 5)

the rise of sophisticated financial instruments.[52] It does not rely on a transaction with an outside insurance company or government agency to secure protection that is expensively underwritten by a bond portfolio.

The federation of the 140 or so UK universities and colleges that form the membership of USS also provides insurance against the systemic risk of a fall in the value of the scheme's growth assets as the result of recession, global financial crisis, pandemic, or the like. Investment risk is spread out temporally across future time-slices of the multigenerational collective body that constitutes a multi-employer LMS scheme. By banding together into a collective pension scheme, consisting of cohorts spanning generations through continual admission of new members, it becomes possible to fill in the shortfalls of those cohorts who live in times when investment returns on growth assets fall short, out of the windfalls of those cohorts who live in times when investment returns rise above the prudently downwardly adjusted best estimate trendline of the discount rate. In adverse scenarios where such smoothing across cohorts proves insufficient, the solution takes the form of extra deficit recovery contributions, consisting of small sums spread over a long period of time, to cover the costs, also spread thinly over time, of paying pensions as they fall due.

The underlying positive cash flow of an open scheme such as USS makes such long, slow amortization possible over multiple decades, in a manner that is not unfair to any particular generation because it thinly spreads the cost over many cohorts. Given the LMS mutuality of USS, and the collective financial strength and longevity of the UK higher education sector, it makes more sense for university employers to cover the pensions of their workers as they fall due, through what is in effect the issuing rather than the purchasing of bonds. As in the case of recent sixty- and 100-year bond issues by Cambridge and Oxford, there would be no need, and it would be self-defeating, to secure these bonds by means of the purchase of equivalent bonds, through the investment of the pension fund in index-linked government and high-quality corporate bonds.

---

[52] In friendly societies of the eighteenth and nineteenth centuries, for example, the costs of risks such as loss of one's capacity to continue to earn a living were shared by all members. Earlier versions of this form of insurance can be found in the food-sharing practices of hunter-gatherers. See Heath, 'The Benefits of Cooperation', pp. 332–4.

This method of underwriting investment risk provides a superior alternative to the requirement to remain within affordable reach of the safe harbour of a bond portfolio. With the insurance underpinning of LMS mutuality, financial assets are freed up for constant and long-term investment in a manner that seeks higher returns, rather than being tied down to the need to provide collateral in the form of liability-matching bonds to secure the pension promises. Because it allows for such long-term investment in growth assets, the insurance of a mutual association is more cost effective than insurance which requires the backing of bonds.

Such mutual insurance also provides a better alternative to the existing UK insurance arrangement to protect DB scheme members in the event of sponsor insolvency. Under this arrangement, each DB sponsor now pays an annual mandatory levy into a government-administered society-wide Pension Protection Fund (PPF). In the event of sponsor insolvency at a time when a scheme's pension fund is insufficient to secure the pension promises, its assets go into the PPF, which then provides most of the promised benefits to members. The PPF invests the levies and assets it receives into a fund that is heavily weighted towards bonds.[53] The rationale for such weighting is that it is necessary to protect the fund from the systemic risk of large numbers of sponsors becoming insolvent at the same time. A crash in the stock market is a systemic risk which pension fund managers face simultaneously. This risk is associated with economic distress which renders it more likely that sponsoring DB employers will become insolvent. The PPF is therefore countercyclically invested in assets such as bonds whose returns are relatively uncorrelated with those of equities.[54] This, however, gives rise to a regulatory demand on pension schemes to be funded to an asset value that does not fall far short of the price of a bond portfolio out of which the pensions promised

---

[53] Under the LMS arrangement, by contrast, if any one employer in the multi-employer scheme becomes insolvent, then, rather than the employer's share of the scheme's assets going into the bond-weighted portfolio of the PPF, it remains within the scheme's fund, which is weighted towards growth assets, to pay for the pensions of all members.

[54] As the PPF explains:

> Our asset allocation is different from the allocations of average defined benefit pension schemes in the UK. This is because we need to be solvent at times when general pension schemes are significantly underfunded. We need a low risk strategy that aims to be relatively uncorrelated to the funding levels of the schemes we protect. (Pension Protection Fund, 'Investment Principles and Strategy')

by insolvent employers who go into the PPF are paid. Otherwise, claims on the PPF might outstrip the assets in that fund. Therefore, this form of insurance ends up providing a version of, rather than an alternative to, an approach to pension funding which is benchmarked to a bond portfolio.

The extension of LMS mutualization across an entire economy of DB schemes would render the PPF and its bond benchmarking redundant, by replacing it with the universal provision of the more cost-effective insurance of a mutual association. There is therefore a sound public policy justification for bringing all employers across society together into a single, large LMS federation to provide affordable, funded pensions on which people can rely in their retirement. The replacement of the PPF with a single, all-encompassing, society-wide LMS federation would provide greater resiliency through diversification than existing LMS arrangements that encompass only a particular sector, industry, or occupational group. Although individual employers and even industries and sectors will come and go, an economy of producers of goods and services is here to stay. We now see that an LMS scheme such as USS can be viewed a model to be generalized across the entire economy of DB schemes. The employer covenant would be rendered strong and endur-ing through the binding together of employers throughout society. The joining together of corporations across society into the mutual associ-ation of such an LMS federation would provide a social union of social unions that extends widely over geographic space, in a manner that underpins the social union of social unions I described at the close of the previous chapter, which extends over time to bind different gener-ations together. The enduring collective entity of an LMS federation would underwrite the risk of investment in growth assets by making it possible to spread the cost of recovery from market downturns over many decades and therefore across generations.

If, however, the current regime of mandatory scheme membership in the PPF were not replaced with a universal mandate to join such an LMS federation, steps would need to be taken to prevent wealthy employers from opting out. Membership in a society-wide LMS feder-ation might be made voluntary, but with extension of tax relief on pension contributions only to those occupational pension schemes that enter into such a multi-employer arrangement. This would provide an incentive for all employers to engage in such risk pooling for mutual advantage. Even when faced with such tax incentives to join together into a multi-employer LMS arrangement, extraordinarily wealthy employers who fear that they will end up the last man standing might still choose to go it alone, as Trinity College Cambridge famously did, when it withdrew in 2019 from USS at significant expense to eliminate the exposure of its asset-rich balance sheet to the risk-sharing mutuality of USS's LMS arrangement.[55]

It is a striking feature of the actuarial advice on which Trinity College chose to withdraw, that a move to a liability-matching portfolio was identified as a major source of risk to the higher education sector. The scenario illustrating the existential threat that USS's LMS arrangement might pose to Trinity College involved the risk of escalating employer contributions caused by the closure of the DB scheme and the subsequent shift of the scheme's assets towards an expensive liability-matching bond portfolio to secure the funding of past pension promises. The increasing cost of funding this portfolio leads to the insolvency of universities, which then drives up the contributions required of the remaining universities, which then leads to further insolvencies, to the point where Trinity College is left the last solvent employer standing.[56] What prompted Trinity College to leave the scheme was not, therefore, the risk the DB scheme posed by remaining open while invested primarily in equities and other growth assets. Rather, it was the risk of the insolvencies of multiple employers caused by the high costs of moving to the 'safe harbour' of a bond portfolio after closure of the scheme.

The USS trustee confirmed Trinity College's fears in its depiction of 'extreme downside scenarios' in which it might call on all employers' available income and assets. These involved circumstances in which USS intervenes to force the sector, at great expense, to purchase a liability-matching bond portfolio. It forces them to do so out of fear that if it does not act soon, the point will be reached where even all the available

---

[55] It is called a 'last man standing' arrangement because, ultimately, the last solvent employer bears responsibility to deliver all the pensions of the members of the scheme in the event of the insolvencies of all the other employers in the scheme.

[56] See XPS Pension, 'Project Bronze'.

income and assets in the higher education sector are insufficient to cover the great cost of such a bond portfolio. USS wrote:

> These scenarios are sufficiently extreme that there is likely to have been institutional failures across a substantial portion of the HE sector. Moreover, in these scenarios the Trustee's call on employers' assets in these scenarios would not necessarily be restrained by the possibility of inflicting additional harm on the HE sector.[57]

This passage implies that USS is prepared to destroy the UK higher education sector to ensure that DB pension promises laid down in the past are paid in full.

Let us grant, if only for the sake of argument, that expensive investment in a liability-matching bond portfolio is the most effective means of securing pension promises that have been laid down in past years. We can also accept, as a matter of current legal fact, that it is a primary duty of the regulator to secure such promises. Nevertheless, the justification of such a duty involves normative considerations of public policy. Such a duty does not follow from any truths in financial economics regarding the proper method of valuing a DB pension liability. Moreover, there cannot be a sound public policy justification for placing so much weight on the securing of past pension promises, even at such high cost, that it undermines the ability of sponsoring employers to make future pension promises, including to the very same workers they have promised pensions in the past, while also threatening the very solvency of such employers and therefore the livelihood of their workers. One will also fail to find a sound justification in moral or legal philosophy for the delivery of promises at such great cost. One might embrace the call to 'Let justice be done, though the heavens may fall.' By contrast, a call to 'Let every DB pension promise be honoured in full though the heavens may fall' is lacking in force. Promises are not absolute. They may be overridden in extremis.[58]

---

[57] USS, 'A Consultation for the 2020 Valuation', p. 16.
[58] The moral justification of a promissory obligation typically involves an appeal to the value of reliance and the harms arising from a failure to meet reasonable expectations. This explains why pension promises should be robust, as people need to rely on them in planning for, and

An abandonment of such an absolutism regarding the delivery of pension promises eliminates the need to fund them in a manner that is benchmarked against a liability-matching bond portfolio. With a weakening of the stringency of the current DB promise, it would be feasible to fund reliable and generous pensions out of the higher returns on growth assets. Owing to the lack of a match between growth assets and pension liabilities, it cannot be guaranteed that it will always be possible to overcome shortfalls in growth assets and pay all promised pensions when they fall due through small increases in contributions over several decades by the many sponsors of an LMS arrangement. In extreme downside scenarios in which absolute pension promises can be met in full only at much greater and more short- and medium-term expense, such promises would be justifiably overridden.

Such an approach converges on the open, ongoing, multigenerational version of a collective defined contribution (CDC) arrangement with which I concluded the previous chapter. There are, in fact, striking respects in which the level of guarantee of the pension that DB schemes provided in the UK prior to the twenty-first century resembles that of CDC. As the name implies, CDC is a type of defined contribution. Like the more familiar individualistic version of defined contribution (IDC), risks are placed on workers rather than employers. But, with CDC, risks are borne by workers collectively rather than individually. As in the case of IDC, the employer's obligation extends no farther than the depositing of a contribution into the pension fund of a given amount in a given year. This contrasts with DB pensions as they are currently regulated in the UK, where employers are often on the hook for onerous deficit recovery contributions to ensure that all pension promises will be honoured in full when they fall due.

The difference traces to the fact that a CDC pension a worker ends up receiving in exchange for his contribution is based upon a target rather than a hard promise of a given amount of pension income in retirement. The target consists of that pension which it will be possible to deliver if,

---

sustaining themselves in, their retirement. It is, however, unreasonable to expect to receive every last penny of pension income that one has been promised, even at the cost of the destruction of higher education opportunities for the next generation.

but only if, investment returns are as good as expected. If investment returns are less good than expected, and hence the targeted pension is underfunded, there is no obligation on the part of the employer to repair the underfunding through extra deficit recovery contributions. Rather, the future or current pension income of workers is adjusted downward, to the point where it can be funded out of the lower than anticipated actual returns. These cuts in pension income might later be restored if returns on investments exceed expectations in later years.

In 1996, the year of the valuation of USS with which I began this chapter, the enforceable obligations of employers to deliver pensions were indistinguishable from their obligations under CDC in the following respect: there was no legal requirement back then to make good any underfunding of an ongoing scheme with extra deficit recovery contributions. Moreover, before 1997, it was possible for the sponsoring employers of DB schemes in the UK to limit their liabilities to the value of the assets in the fund simply by winding up the scheme at any time. If these assets were insufficient to pay all pensions that had been promised up to that point of termination of the scheme, some members would end up receiving less than the pensions they had been promised.[59] In some instances, the shortfall in receipt compared to what they had been promised was considerable.

Today, the situation is very different. In the early to mid-2000s, regulations came into force which require solvent sponsoring employers who wind up their DB scheme to secure the pension liabilities of all members by paying a sum of money sufficient to cover the cost of purchase of matching annuities from an insurance company, where this cost approximates the yield on long-dated government bonds. The PPF was also created, to compensate scheme members for loss of their pensions when their employers become insolvent while lacking sufficient means to buy out their DB liabilities through an insurance company or otherwise pay all pensions as they fall due. As discussed above, this Fund is financed by levies assessed on all schemes, which are invested in a portfolio weighted towards bonds.

These forms of protection against loss of promised DB pensions all involve backstops that secure these promises out of liability-matching

---

[59] See Blake, *Pension Schemes and Pension Funds*, p. 105.

bond portfolios. In line with this fact as well as its formal objectives, the regulator seeks to ensure that the funding of DB schemes never falls too far short of the cost of purchasing such a bond portfolio in the event that an employer becomes weak or insolvent at the same time that the returns on the assets in their DB schemes are less than expected.

The contrasting approach of the 1990s to funding DB schemes out of lower contributions, with greater reliance on the higher expected returns of growth assets, makes good sense only in the absence of the legal protections of pensions that have arisen since then. We cannot return to those days of lower contributions and reliance on higher returns from growth assets, without also forgoing the bond-based protections of pension promises that have arisen since then. We cannot have our cake and eat it too, where the cake is lower contributions combined with reliance on higher expected returns on growth assets, and eating it too is the bond-underpinned legal protection of these promises.

Those who would like to return to the heyday of private sector DB pension provision in the UK, which spanned the last four decades of the last century, should welcome a transformation of today's DB into something that at least converges on and approximates CDC. This is because, by reaping higher returns on lower contributions, the latter is likely to provide—but does not and cannot absolutely guarantee—the generous pensions that people received, but were not guaranteed, back then. The heyday of defined benefit was, in essence even if not in name, an age of collective defined contribution. CDC will not, however, constitute a mere repetition of history. The aforementioned power of trustees back then to wind up the scheme at any point in time left members vulnerable to the possibility of a drastic cut in their pension overnight. Under both current regulations and Royal Mail's scheme design, by contrast, the pensions of members will be far more resilient to scheme closure.[60] The shaping of the regulation and practice of CDC in the UK has been informed by the mistakes as well as the successes of the past.

---

[60] Recall from the discussion in Chapter 1 that Royal Mail's scheme has been designed to make it possible, by means of gradual transformation from CDC to collective individual defined contribution (CIDC), to provide generous pensions even if the scheme closes to new members.

3

The Case for an Unfunded Pay as You Go Pension

The previous two chapters were devoted entirely to a consideration of pensions that are funded. A *funded* pension is one in which your pension is drawn from the realization of returns on the investment of contributions into a pension fund that typically both you and your employer have made during your working life. This fund might be held by just you as an individual, as in the case of a traditional individual defined contribution (DC) pension pot, which I discussed in Chapter 1. Or the fund might be held collectively with others, with whom one pools risks. Collective defined contribution (CDC), which was the topic of my first chapter, and the funded occupational defined benefit (DB) pension scheme, which was the topic of my second chapter, each involve collective funding.[1]

Investment risk poses perhaps the greatest challenge for funded pensions. Especially in recent years of historically low bond yields, the low-risk option of investment in long-dated inflation-linked government bonds that match the pension liabilities has been prohibitively expensive. In order, however, to reap the premium of higher expected returns on equities and property, one must contend with the risk that these returns

---

[1] Joseph Heath has argued that individual defined contribution (IDC) pension pots are not fundamentally different from PAYG DB pension schemes. In making this argument, he appeals to the fact that the money in one's IDC pension pot is itself a set of promises in the form of IOUs. (See 'The Structure of Intergenerational Cooperation', p. 61.) I agree with Heath that money is nothing but promissory notes, while pointing to the following significant difference that remains between the money in one's IDC pension pot and a DB pension scheme: the latter involves a promise on the part of the underwriting institution to deliver income of a given level from one's retirement to death. This is true whether the DB pension scheme is funded or PAYG. The money in one's pension pot might be exchanged for such a promise via purchase of an annuity from an insurance company. But, absent such an exchange, it falls short of a DB pension promise.

How to Pool Risks across Generations: The Case for Collective Pensions. Michael Otsuka, Oxford University Press.
© Michael Otsuka 2023. DOI: 10.1093/oso/9780198885962.003.0004

will fall far short of expectation. In the previous two chapters, I considered several different ways in which individuals and collectives might try to manage these risks. Needless to say, none of them provides a foolproof method of dealing with the uncertainty of returns on investment.

In light of the problems to which investment risk gives rise, it is worthwhile to consider the merits and promise of another form of pension provision, which does not involve the investment of contributions that have been deposited into a pension fund. In this chapter, I shall consider the case for pensions that are provided on an unfunded 'pay as you go' (PAYG) basis. With a PAYG scheme, money is transferred from those who are currently working to pay the pensions of those who are currently retired. Like many other state pensions, those in the USA and the UK are PAYG. Rather than drawing from a pension fund consisting of a portfolio of financial assets, US and UK state pensions are paid out of annual tax revenues or government borrowing. The pension one is entitled to in retirement is, however, based on, even though not funded by, the contributions one has made during one's working life in the form of a payroll tax. In some other countries, neither eligibility for the basic PAYG state pension nor its level is conditional on contributions of portions of one's earnings during one's working life. These arrangements are more akin to other forms of welfare spending involving redistributive transfers funded solely by general taxation. There remains a non-contributory residency requirement for eligibility, as in the case of other forms of welfare spending. In some cases, there is merely a threshold residency requirement: all who have lived for a given number of years are eligible to the same degree. In the Netherlands, the residency requirement is scalar rather than a threshold: the level of the basic state pension to which one is entitled increases on the basis of the number of years that one has been a resident.

Many public sector occupational pensions are also PAYG. In the UK, the pensions of National Health Service workers, civil servants, and members of the armed forces are provided on an unfunded PAYG basis. The Teachers' Pension Scheme in the UK is another example. It is of special relevance as a benchmark of comparison with the Universities Superannuation Scheme (USS) because, alongside teachers in primary and secondary schools, instructors in most of the universities that have been established since 1992 are also members of the PAYG scheme. In these public sector schemes, employees and employers make contributions along the lines of private sector occupational schemes. But these contributions go into the coffers of the state Treasury rather than being invested in a portfolio of assets in a fund. Pension payments also come from the Treasury's coffers.

An unfunded PAYG state pension can be justified as a means to redistribute income from those who have the good fortune to be higher earners to those who suffer the misfortune of lower earnings, where such redistribution cannot be achieved by means of the risk pooling of the earnings of different people that is in the actual *ex ante* self-interest of all who enter the pool. In other words, unfunded PAYG can be justified when we require the services of Robin Hood and not just the insurance of a mutual association. Like a number of other unfunded PAYG state pensions, the UK state pension is, in fact, highly redistributive. The amount that one contributes is proportional to one's income, up to an income ceiling. But the level of one's annual pension in retirement is proportional simply to the number of years one has worked and made mandatory contributions on income that exceeds a low threshold. Hence, money is transferred from high earners to low earners, with the goal of relieving poverty in old age, on what has come to be known as the Beveridge as opposed to the Bismarck approach to state pensions.[2]

Such an arrangement would probably not be in the actual *ex ante* self-interest of each to adopt, at the point at which one leaves full-time education and begins one's working career. This is because, even at that early point, each person has a fairly good idea of whether his expected earnings will be high or low. It would probably not therefore be in the rational self-interest of those who expect to be higher earners to choose a state pension along UK lines. One would need to impose a thicker hypothetical veil, which deprives people of knowledge of their

---

[2] On the Bismarck approach, both pensions and contributions are proportional to earnings, whereas on the Beveridge approach the level of the pensions people receive is set to keep pensioners out of poverty and is relatively insensitive to people's earnings and the size of their contributions. Private occupational DB pensions are almost invariably contributory along Bismarckian lines.

talents, and therefore their earning potential, to render it in the rational self-interest of each to choose such a redistributive state pension at the beginning of his adult life. A Dworkinian luck egalitarian would offer just such a justification, grounded in hypothetical insurance choices, for an unfunded, redistributive PAYG state pension.[3]

In this chapter, I shall address the question of whether there is a *reciprocity-based*, as distinct from a redistributive, justification for an unfunded PAYG pension such as the US or the UK state pension. In particular, might such an arrangement provide a realization of reciprocity in the Rawlsian sense of fair terms of social cooperation for mutual advantage, which he situates as follows between altruistic impartiality and mere mutual advantage?

> the idea of reciprocity lies between the idea of impartiality, which is altruistic (being moved by the general good), and the idea of mutual advantage understood as everyone's being advantaged with respect to each person's present or expected future situation as things are. As understood in justice as fairness, reciprocity is a relation between citizens expressed by principles of justice that regulate a social world in which everyone benefits judged with respect to an appropriate benchmark of equality defined with respect to that world.[4]

The fact that people would prudently select a redistributive PAYG state pension from behind a hypothetical veil of ignorance is, I think, insufficient to establish that it embodies the idea of reciprocity. There are the following reasons why it is hard to interpret Rawlsian self-interested choice behind a veil of ignorance as involving reciprocity. First, it does not involve an agreement, or even tit-for-tat interaction, between different individuals. Rather, it involves the self-interested choice of a single individual.[5] Second, the choice is self-interested only on the hypothetical assumption that the individual might turn out to be any member of society.

---

[3] See Dworkin, *Justice for Hedgehogs*, pp. 360–1, and *Sovereign Virtue*, chs. 2 and 9.
[4] Rawls, *Political Liberalism*, pp. 16–17.   [5] See Hampton, 'Contracts and Choices'.

To elaborate on this second point: The choice is not in everyone's actual self-interest. Moreover, it is in everyone's *ex ante* self-interest only by virtue of the imposition of a veil that strips one of one's knowledge of one's particular fate or prospects. Consideration of the following example reveals why this fact undermines the case for reciprocity. Suppose that there are a number of young adults, each of whom knows that he is suffering from a congenital illness. Half know that they are suffering from an illness that will cause their death at the age of 30 if untreated, and the other half know that they are suffering from a different congenital illness that will cause their death at the age of 50 if untreated. On account of scarcity of resources and therefore the limits to the revenue that can be raised from the taxation of the fruits of social cooperation, the National Health Service is able to treat only one of these ailments. Treatment would, in either case, result in a healthy life to the age of 80 for all who receive it. If these individuals are placed behind a veil of ignorance, which renders it rational for each to assume that he has an equal probability of suffering either illness, it will be in the *ex ante* self-interest of each to choose that the treatment goes to those who would die at 30 rather than those who would die at 50.

If we regard choice from behind the veil as providing the benchmark of equality, and if we regard the maximization of one's expected utility as a benefit, then the conditions for Rawlsian reciprocity will have been met. It is, however, only in an artificially stretched sense that the choice of the treatment for those who would die at 30 is to the mutual advantage of each. This is a stretch given both that such treatment is to the actual advantage, *ex post*, of only half of the population and that it is to the *ex ante* expected advantage of each only when nobody knows who he is. The normative appeal of the claim that the chosen option is to the advantage of each is undermined if we can provide such a justification only by depriving people of knowledge of who in particular they are.

Rawls maintains that his original position models 'a fair system of cooperation for mutual advantage between free and equal persons'.[6] On account of the impartiality of the choice that the veil insures among symmetrically situated individuals, what would be chosen in the original

---

[6] 'Justice as Fairness: Political, not Metaphysical', p. 241.

position might constitute a fair system of cooperation among equals. But, as we have just seen, it might not be to the mutual advantage of each, and we should not be misled by the fact that Rawls's modelling involves self-interested choice into thinking that the terms of cooperation chosen in the original position are in fact mutually advantageous. Such choice behind the veil might be better understood as modelling impartial altruism rather than reciprocity.[7]

We should see whether we can provide an account of the reciprocity of a PAYG pension scheme, which does not require the hypothetical imposition of a veil to demonstrate the mutually advantageous nature of the scheme.

Worker contributions that pay for the pensions of those in retirement in an unfunded PAYG scheme are not in return for benefits that those in retirement confer on this group of workers.[8] They therefore differ from the typical bidirectional form of reciprocity in which parties exchange benefits with one another. One might, however, try to draw an analogy between PAYG and other intergenerational arrangements, where the latter are plausibly characterized as reciprocal even though they are unidirectional in nature rather than involving a bidirectional exchange.

Rawls's just savings principle might provide such an analogy. Rawls maintains that since 'generations are spread out in time and actual economic benefits flow only in one direction', there 'is no way for later generations to help the situation of the least fortunate earlier generation' when these generations are non-overlapping.[9] Each generation therefore benefits the next generation by saving for it, but not in exchange for any benefit that the next generation confers on it.[10] In spite of its

---

[7] Rawls, in fact, notes that 'the combination of mutual disinterest and the veil of ignorance achieves much the same purpose as benevolence [without the veil]. For this combination of conditions forces each person in the original position to take the good of others into account' (*Theory of Justice*, pp. 128–9).

[8] I set to one side the possibility that these worker contributions are to be conceived as in return for the taxes that pensioners paid when they were workers, for the education of workers when they were children.

[9] *Theory of Justice*, p. 254.

[10] Generations do not literally pass along savings in the manner of bequests of bank accounts. Rather, they divide their activities between the production of consumption goods and invest-ment goods. 'Savings' consist of the pool of capital available for production of investment goods. It is these investment or capital goods that are passed along to the next generation. Thus,

unidirectional nature, a case can be made that Rawls's just savings principle is grounded in a principle of reciprocity involving the notion of fair return to a party other than the one from which one has received a benefit. Rather, any given generation is obliged to benefit the next generation in return for a benefit it has received from the *previous* generation.

Rawls's own argument for his just savings principle involves an appeal to a principle of universalizability rather than reciprocity.[11] From behind the veil, we choose a savings principle for our own (unknown) generation on the assumption that all previous and future generations adopt the same principle: 'the correct principle is that which the members of any generation (and so all generations) would adopt as the one their generation is to follow and as the principle they would want preceding generations to have followed (and later generations to follow), no matter how far back (or forward) in time'.[12] Among the requirements of this principle are that each generation saves for the next at least as much as the previous generation saved for it.[13]

Alternatively, one might try to defend Rawls's just savings principle by means of an appeal to his principle of fairness, according to which one has an obligation to contribute to a cooperative scheme that is triggered by the benefits one has received from that scheme.[14] A just savings principle might be conceived as a form of cooperation insofar as it is to the mutual advantage of each. Along these lines, Rawls writes: 'if all generations are to gain (except perhaps the earlier ones), the parties must agree to a savings principle that insures that each generation receives its due from its predecessor and does its fair share for those to come'.[15] Perhaps the charge of free-riding off the efforts of others that is integral

intergenerational defection would take the form of a failure to replenish the capital stock: i.e., failure to maintain infrastructure, failure to build new machines, etc. (I am indebted to an anonymous reader for this point and its spelling out.)

[11] Brian Barry interprets Rawls as appealing to a principle of universalizability. See Barry, *Theories of Justice*, p. 197.

[12] Rawls, *Political Liberalism*, p. 274.   [13] Rawls, *Theory of Justice*, p. 256.

[14] For Rawls's version of the principle of fairness, see *Theory of Justice*, pp. 96–8 and §52. Barry argues that Rawls's just savings principle can be justified via appeal to the principle of fair play. The principle that Barry invokes, however, is not Rawls's principle of fairness, but rather Rawls's 'natural duty to uphold and further just institutions'. See Barry, *Theories of Justice*, p. 201.

[15] *Theory of Justice*, p. 254.

to the principle of fairness can be invoked to condemn those who benefit from the savings of their ancestors without in turn passing on comparable savings to their descendants. Although this would not involve an appeal to reciprocity in the ordinary sense involving bidirectional exchanges, it might be thought to involve a version of reciprocity, more widely understood.

There is, however, the following disanalogy between Rawls's just savings principle and PAYG. A PAYG pension scheme differs, in the order in which benefits are received and contributions are made, from an arrangement in which each past generation saves for the next generation. In the case of savings, the members of one generation receive a benefit from the previous generation, which might plausibly be thought to generate a duty of fairness to provide a comparable benefit to the next generation. A PAYG scheme, however, reverses the direction of benefits: workers of the current generation G_n *provide* benefits to retirees of the previous (partially overlapping) generation G_{n-1}, which is meant to give rise to an obligation on the part of workers of the next generation G_{n+1} to provide benefits to workers of the current generation G_n when they retire. But why, one might ask, should the fact that members of G_n have provided benefits to members of the previous generation G_{n-1} give rise to an obligation of *fairness* on the part of members of G_{n+1} to provide benefits to members of G_n (and members of G_{n+2} to provide benefits to members of G_{n+1}, etc.)? At the point at which they are allegedly obliged to contribute to the retirement of members of G_n, members of G_{n+1} have not yet benefited from anyone else's contributions and will never receive pension benefits from the members of either G_n or G_{n-1}.

One can respond to this challenge by drawing attention to the fact that members of G_{n+1} (and others) might each benefit from general conformity to a norm which calls for the provision of such benefits. A world in which each conforms to such a norm might be better for each than a world in which nobody conforms, but rather each person hoards benefits for himself rather than giving anything to anyone else. Moreover, a norm whereby G_n's benefiting G_{n-1} gives rise to an obligation that G_{n+1} benefit G_n, that G_{n+2} benefit G_{n+1}, and so forth, might arise and persist because conformity to it gives rise to a strategic equilibrium in which each does better for oneself by conforming rather than defecting, given the choices of others.

In a manner analogous to that of an unfunded PAYG pension scheme, but at the level of individual members of a family across overlapping generations, Ken Binmore has argued that conformity to a norm of benefiting one's elders might be such a mutually advantageous strategic equilibrium. He asks us to

> imagine a world in which only a mother and a daughter are alive at any time. Each player lives for two periods. The first period is her youth, and the second her old age. In her youth, a player bakes two (large) loaves of bread. She then gives birth to a daughter, and immediately grows old. Old players are too feeble to work, and so produce nothing. One equilibrium requires each player to consume both her loaves of bread in her youth. Everyone will then have to endure a miserable old age, but everyone will be optimizing given the choices of the others. All players would prefer to consume one loaf in their youth and one loaf in their old age. But this "fair" outcome can only be achieved if the daughters all give one of their two loaves to their mothers, because bread perishes if not consumed when baked.[16]

A world in which each conforms to a norm of sharing with one's elder is better for each than a world in which nobody conforms, but rather each person hoards benefits for herself rather than giving anything to anyone else.

Binmore offers the following explanation of how conformity to a norm of sharing might emerge:

> Mothers can't retaliate if their daughters are selfish, but the fair outcome can nevertheless be sustained as an equilibrium. In this fair equilibrium, a conformist is a player who gives her mother a loaf if and only if her mother was a conformist in her youth. Conformists therefore reward other conformists, and punish nonconformists.

---

[16] Binmore, *Natural Justice*, p. 87.

To see why a daughter gives her mother a loaf, suppose that Alice, Beatrice, and Carol are mother, daughter, and granddaughter. If Beatrice neglects Alice, she becomes a nonconformist. Carol therefore punishes Beatrice, to avoid becoming a nonconformist herself. If not, she will be punished by her daughter—and so on. If the first-born player is deemed to be a conformist, it is therefore a perfect equilibrium for everybody to be a conformist.[17]

Joseph Heath employs a similar model to make the case that unfunded PAYG pension schemes embody a form of indirect reciprocity involving intergenerational cooperation where benefits flow in one direction only. Workers of one generation pay for the pensions of those in retirement at that time, in return for having their pensions paid by the next generation of workers when they are retired. He describes the motivation to participate in and contribute to a PAYG university pension in the following terms:

> It is because I am confident that when I am older and retired there will be a new generation of young professors who are willing to do the same thing for me that I am currently doing for my emeritus colleagues. But why should I expect the next generation to be willing to hand over 5 percent of their salary to me? Certainly not out of gratitude for the fact that I am doing so now, to the benefit of my older colleagues. It is because I expect them to expect that they will someday have younger colleagues who will do the same for them, that is, that the chain of cooperation will continue on into the future unbroken (or that the pension scheme will remain, as they say, a "going concern").[18]

The reciprocity involved in a decision to join and contribute to such a PAYG scheme differs from that which underpins a decision to purchase an annuity from an insurance company. The latter involves the more familiar bidirectional reciprocity of a legally binding contract: I agree to part with a large sum of money up front in exchange for a guarantee

---

[17] Binmore, *Natural Justice*, p. 87.
[18] 'The Structure of Intergenerational Cooperation', p. 50.

from the insurance company to pay me small sums of money over time from point of retirement to death. Here the guarantee is underpinned by capital requirements involving the backing of a bond portfolio which provides me with the assurance that this promise will be delivered even if the insurance company is no longer trading during my retirement.[19] In the case of a DB scheme involving a hard promise funded by a 'liability-matching' bond portfolio, a similar form of bidirectional reciprocity might be sufficient to explain a worker's motivation to join such a scheme. Such funding provides the worker with the assurance that her promise will be delivered in retirement even if the scheme has been wound up and there are no younger workers contributing into the scheme at that point. Bond-based funding is, however, more expensive than funding backed by growth assets. It requires greater contributions up front to provide a given level of pension income in retirement.[20] It is also more expensive than a PAYG pension. Moreover, in the cases of both PAYG and an ongoing DB scheme funded from growth assets, the expectation that the scheme will remain a going concern—that it will remain open to new members who will continue to pay into it through-out the retirements of older members—is necessary to justify one's joining and remaining a member of the scheme. Hence both sorts of arrangements involve the expectation of a reciprocity that is indirect rather than bidirectional.

Does such an expectation that the next generation of workers will contribute during their retirements, because they expect the generation afterwards to contribute during their retirements, and so forth, also explain why today's workers contribute to a state PAYG pension? One might think the answer is 'No' in this case, given the mandatory nature of the contribution, along the lines of a legally enforceable income tax. Here the automatic nature of the payroll deduction, combined with the fear of punishment for evading such contributions, can provide the full explan-ation for why individuals contribute to such a scheme.

A norm in strategic equilibrium of the sort that Binmore describes might, however, play a role in explaining how state pensions are sustained

---

[19] See my discussion of an insurance company annuity in Chapter 1.
[20] See my discussion in Chapter 2 of these different approaches to funding a DB pension.

over time, by means of the collective decisions of voters rather than at the level of the contributions of individuals. State pension contributions are mandatory. But the state pension is not underpinned by a bilateral and legally enforceable reciprocal contract between the state and the individual whereby the state promises anyone a given level of pension in exchange for that individual's contributions. Rather, the state pension can be altered at democratic will, and hence what people end up being paid in retirement is not guaranteed or otherwise fixed in advance. The fact, however, that voters do not elect to stop paying for and close down a PAYG state pension might be explained by the following strategic equilibrium at the level of the collective: voters democratically choose to continue to require contributions to pay for the pensions of those in retirement, not just because the elderly vote in disproportionate numbers, but because workers realize that if they vote to stop making contributions towards the pensions of those in retirement, then the next generation of workers will vote against making contributions towards *their* retirement. Here the enforcement mechanism is along the lines that Binmore describes in the second quoted passage above.

Assuming that the members of the different generations are equally situated, this mutually advantageous strategic equilibrium might be described as an instance of the type of Rawlsian reciprocity that I introduced above: one which involves 'a relation between citizens expressed by principles of justice that regulate a social world in which everyone benefits judged with respect to an appropriate benchmark of equality'.[21] Here, as in Binmore's mother–daughter example, each generation benefits by having another generation provide for their retirement, rather than having to provide for their own retirement. As we shall see in a moment, however, the assumption that the members of the different generations of a PAYG scheme are equally situated is unsound. The first generation is privileged over the others, and hence we do not have the requisite benchmark of equality.[22]

---

[21] *Political Liberalism*, p. 17.
[22] Assuming that Binmore's scenario includes an original Eve who receives a loaf from her daughter even though she has no mother to whom to provide a loaf, not all parties are equally situated in his case either, since Eve will enjoy a windfall, relative to the others.

Unfunded PAYG state pensions involve the prima facie unfairness of the first generation's getting a free ride, since they made few if any contributions into the system.[23] The first American, for example, to receive a monthly social security cheque had paid only $24.75 in contributions over three years when she received her first monthly cheque of $22.54 at the age of 65 in 1940. She ultimately collected a total of $22,888.92 during the ensuing thirty-five years, leading up to her death at the age of 100.[24]

In theory, we could construct an almost entirely unfunded PAYG state pension scheme in which members of the first generation to receive a pension in retirement make contributions into the scheme throughout their working lives. Unlike a normal PAYG scheme, these contributions would not go towards any pensions in payment at the time, since, by hypothesis, there would be none. If these contributions were instead invested, ring-fenced, and held in reserve for the payment of their own future pensions, and the same arrangement was applied to all subsequent generations, this would transform the arrangement into a funded pension scheme. Suppose, by contrast, that the pension contributions of the first generation were instead invested, ring-fenced, and held in reserve to pay the pensions for the retirement of the *final* generation of those who contributed during their working lives, in the event of eventual scheme closure. In this case, all generations would be equally situated insofar as each generation which receives a pension would also make contributions that pay the pensions of another generation. Here each generation would pay the pensions of the previous generation in typical unfunded PAYG fashion, *except* for the first generation, whose contributions would loop forward to the final generation. Apart from the fact that the first generation's contributions would be held and invested in a fund for the last generation, this would be an unfunded PAYG realization of an indirect form of Rawlsian reciprocity. Reciprocity arises here from a benchmark of equality, since each generation both contributes to another generation's pension and receives contributions for its own pension from

---

[23] This problem also crops up in Heath's modelling of 'indirect reciprocity' with overlapping generations. See 'The Structure of Intergenerational Cooperation', pp. 46–7.

[24] See DeWitt, 'Details of Ida May Fuller's Payroll Tax Contributions'.

another generation.[25] This is, however, merely an interesting theoretical possibility. No actually existing PAYG state pension scheme has ever involved such a looping forward arrangement, nor is its future implementation likely.

This merely theoretically interesting possibility does, however, set the stage for the consideration of another version of PAYG which realizes reciprocity insofar as each generation both fully contributes to, and receives from, an ongoing pension scheme. This PAYG arrangement involves the *notional* funding of all pension promises, including those of the first generation of pensioners. It is not merely an interesting theoretical possibility, as it has been realized in actual practice. On account of its merits, I shall turn to a consideration of it for the remainder of this chapter.

As in the case of a genuinely funded DB pension scheme, workers and employers in a notionally funded PAYG scheme put in pension contributions each year, in return for which workers are promised a pension in retirement. The pensions of every scheme member, including those of the very first generation, are directly proportional to the level of their contributions throughout their working lives. Therefore, the first generation of pensioners does not ride free on the contributions of younger workers. The complaint I raised above against PAYG state pensions does not apply here.[26]

UK public sector PAYG pension schemes provide a good example of how such notional funding works in practice. The cost of the pensions that public sector workers are promised is covered by the contributions

---

[25] This looping arrangement would also provide a solution to the following problem of backward induction that has been pressed against PAYG schemes. If there is a known future date at which a PAYG pension scheme will close with no further payments of pensions, the members of the generation who know they will retire at or near the date of closure will refuse to contribute during their working lives to the pensions of the members of the previous generation. But then, knowing that they too will not receive pensions, the members of that previous generation will refuse to contribute to the pensions of the members of the generation before them. And so forth. For a discussion of this problem, see Heath, 'The Structure of Intergenerational Cooperation', pp. 54–6.

[26] We will not get around the problem of backward induction mentioned above if members of the first generation of pensioners pay merely notional contributions, which are not invested and ring-fenced for the last generation. But, setting this problem to one side (e.g., by assuming that the scheme never closes), these notional contributions will secure reciprocity insofar as everyone who receives a pension will also have contributed, even if these contributions do not actually fund their own pensions.

of employers and members plus an assumed rate of return on these contributions. This assumed return also serves as the rate at which the pension liabilities are discounted: the discount rate. As in the case of a genuinely funded DB pension, the higher this assumed rate of return, the lower the contributions required to provide a pension of a given level. Here, however, the funding is merely notional, rather than actual, since contributions are not deposited into a ring-fenced fund which is invested in financial assets. Rather, they go into the coffers of the state Treasury.

The notional rate of return is set, not as the expected rate of return r on the capital of a hypothetical portfolio of financial assets, but rather as the expected long-term rate of growth g of the economy (gross domestic product). The rationale for setting the discount rate as g is that PAYG pensions are funded by tax revenues, which grow roughly in line with the growth in the economy. Hence the hypothetical 'assets' of the scheme are metaphorically conceived as 'claims on future tax revenue'. As the Treasury has explained:

> the Government is not persuaded that a rate consistent with the private sector and other funded schemes would be an appropriate choice as the discount rate used to set unfunded pension scheme contributions. It [the former discount rate] reflects the costs inherent in a scheme backed by a portfolio of assets (traded bonds and equities) not held by the unfunded public service schemes (whose assets are claims on future tax revenues).[27]

In setting the rate of return on pension contributions as the rate at which tax revenues are expected to grow, the Treasury maintained that they thereby 'take into account the costs passed to future taxpayers on a fair and sustainable basis'.[28]

There are efficiency-based grounds for preferring a PAYG to a genuinely funded pension scheme, such as the low cost of administration in

---

[27] See Treasury, 'Consultation on the Discount Rate', sec. 3.29. See also secs. 3.15–3.18 and 3.28–3.32.

[28] Treasury, 'Update'. According to the Treasury, to set the discount rate as higher than g would give rise 'to a disproportionate increase in the claims on future tax income, which was considered inequitable' ('Consultation on the Discount Rate', sec. 3.25).

contrast to the relatively high cost of good management of the portfolio of assets of a funded pension scheme.[29] A case for a notionally funded PAYG pension might be especially strong when $g>r$, where g represents the rate of *per capita* as opposed to aggregate growth of the economy.[30] In that case, it should be possible to provide better pensions for all via a notionally funded PAYG scheme in which pensions are paid out of tax revenues that increase at the rate of g, as compared with a genuinely funded scheme whose assets grow at the lower rate of return on capital r. Such a notionally funded PAYG scheme could be justified as to the reciprocal mutual advantage of each, in comparison with a genuinely funded scheme.

If, however, Thomas Piketty is right that it was an aberration that $g>r$ during the twentieth century, and $r>g$ is the historical norm, that would undermine such an efficiency-based case for PAYG over funded provision of pension promises in future years.[31] It would undermine but not defeat the case for PAYG since, as I hope now to show, a case for PAYG can be made even when $r>g$, which is to say even when the rate of return on capital exceeds the rate of growth of the economy.

To make this case, I shall begin by drawing attention to some striking parallels between a notionally funded PAYG DB scheme and a genuinely funded one, which shed light on what a notionally funded PAYG pension actually consists of and when the case for it will be compelling. As I mentioned in Chapter 2, some people maintain that DB schemes should invest in long-dated inflation-index-linked government bonds to ensure that the assets in their fund 'match' the liabilities of their pension promises. I made the case there for a less expensive funding by means of investment in growth assets. I would like to make a different point here: namely, that pension contributions for a notionally funded

---

[29] These are localized costs borne by the members and sponsors of the particular pension scheme. There are also non-localized macroeconomic costs and benefits associated with having so much wealth invested in pension funds. Optimal investment from a local perspective might be sub-optimal—e.g., pro-cyclical, or involving underinvestment in productive assets—from a macroeconomic perspective.

[30] For more on the superiority of PAYG to funded pensions when $g>r$, see Wren-Lewis, 'Unfunded Pension Schemes and Intergenerational Equity'.

[31] See Piketty, *Capital in the Twenty-first Century*. For confirmation of Piketty, see Jordà et al., 'The Rate of Return on Everything'. For a contrasting view, see Schmelzing, 'Eight Centuries of Global Real Interest Rates'.

PAYG scheme constitute the purchase of government bonds. In exchange for employer and member contributions that go into the state Treasury's coffers, the government makes promises to pay pensions. Such promises amount to illiquid (non-tradeable) government annuity bonds. The yield of these annuity bonds is the discount rate g, which is the rate of return on the contributions. As I mentioned above, for UK public sector schemes, this is set as the long-term rate of growth of the economy, which was assumed to be CPI+2.4% under the discount rate in force from 2018 to the present.[32] Such annuity bonds provide an attractive yield, relative to the long-dated inflation-indexed bonds that the government issues, whose returns have been negative in real terms in recent years. If such annuity bonds were publicly tradeable, funded DB pension schemes alone would create enormous demand for them.[33] Therefore, PAYG public sector schemes in the UK are in effect government-bond-funded schemes, but with a better yield of CPI+2.4% than that of the long-dated index-linked bonds which some financial economists maintain should largely constitute the portfolios of privately funded DB pensions.

A yield of CPI+2.4% is not as high as the expected long-term return on equities, which is now in the vicinity of CPI+4%. But, unlike in the case of equities investment, there is no risk to the asset-holder: the employers and members who pay the contributions in exchange for the government-issued annuities do not bear any investment risk. Should a pension scheme prefer to invest more cheaply in risky equities with a higher expected return or in government annuities that have a rate of return pegged to the forecast growth of the economy? Rather than expose themselves to the downside risk of equities, I'm sure that many would leap at the chance to purchase liability-matching assets with a government-guaranteed return of CPI+2.4%.[34]

---

[32] See Treasury, 'Public Service Pensions', p. 14.

[33] Such demand would greatly increase the price of, and therefore decrease the yield on, these bonds, to something closer to those of long-dated inflation-linked government bonds. The price of the latter would, however, go down and their yield would go up, on account of the decrease in demand for them among pension funds, as they switch over to the more closely matching government annuity bonds I've just been describing.

[34] They would likely leap at this chance even bearing in mind that this rate will change in future years with changes in forecasts of the growth of the economy. One reason to opt for these annuity bonds even though their yield may change in future is that, unlike a change in the yield

Issues of fairness might therefore be thought to arise, on account of the fact that the UK government now issues and exclusively sells annuity bonds at well below their fair market value, to only some workers and employers: namely, those who qualify for membership in public sector PAYG schemes. What grounds are there for the state to make these bonds available for purchase by those in the public sector but not the private sector? To overcome a charge of partiality and unfairness, these annuity bonds could be made available to all employers and workers, including those in the private as well as the public sector.

Here is a related question for those who call for private sector DB pensions to be funded out of a portfolio of long-dated inflation-index-linked government bonds: what explains your preference for funding such pensions at the lower discount rate of such government bonds rather than the higher discount rate of the annuity bonds the government makes available to public sector workers?

Is it because this lower rate reflects the value of the promises to workers and pensioners, as revealed by an indifference between their promised pensions and such liability-matching government bonds, and hence a willingness to trade the one for the other? This answer would repeat a mistake along the lines of the one I identified in Chapter 2 of confusing the exchange value of a pension with the funding required to secure its provision. In its rejection of the index-linked bond yield as the discount rate for PAYG pensions, the Treasury noted that 'this option in effect answers a slightly different question' from that of what the discount rate should be for setting the level of required contributions and funding: namely, 'what would be the cost to an individual of buying a funded pension pot with the same characteristics as an unfunded public service pension scheme?'[35]

Is it because the yield on long-dated index-linked bonds is set by the free market, whereas the CPI + 2.4% yield of annuity bonds is the product

---

of bonds in the portfolio of a funded scheme, this change would not make a difference to the assessed cost of past promises. It would only increase the cost of making pension promises in future years. A further reason to opt for such annuity bonds is that a decrease in the expected growth of the economy would likely correlate with a decrease in the expected long-term return on equities, and hence the alternative of investment in equities would also become less attractive.

[35] 'Consultation on the Discount Rate', sec. 3.12.

of an unfree market, given restrictions on who can purchase them and the inability to trade them? But of course the market that determines yields on long-dated index-linked bonds is far from free of government influence, given the high dependence of such yields on Bank of England decisions to raise or lower the base rate to meet its inflation target. The government has become an especially outsized player in bond markets as a result of the adoption in recent years of a policy of quantitative easing. Bond yields were driven down on account of the central bank's injection of money into the economy, involving the buying back of government bonds held by insurance companies, pension funds, banks, and other institutions.

It is ultimately a matter of choice on the part of the government what sorts of bonds to issue and to whom. Though this might have undesirable effects which would tell against doing so—such as inflation or the crowding out of government borrowing for investment in infrastructure and the like—the government can choose to issue CPI+2.4% annuity bonds in greater volume and to make them more widely available to workers and employers.

At the close of Chapter 2, I showed how CDC converges on DB. I have now shown how notionally funded PAYG DB also converges on funded DB. Climbing the mountain from different sides, each of these approaches reaches a similar form of collective pension provision, which breaks open the silos of individual DC pension pots and avoids the higher expense of funding that is pegged to long-dated index-linked government bonds. Whether it ultimately takes the form of CDC, a genuinely funded DB scheme, or a notionally funded PAYG DB scheme, we have arrived at a collective, multigenerational, society-wide form of pension provision.

4

Fair Terms of Social Cooperation among the Free and Equal

According to Rawls, the 'first fundamental question' of justice concerns the specification of 'the fair terms of social cooperation between citizens regarded as free and equal, and as fully cooperating members of society over a complete life, from one generation to the next'.[1] In previous chapters, this idea of fair terms of cooperation for mutual advantage has figured prominently in the case I have constructed for collective pensions, which involve the cooperation over the life cycles of overlapping generations, by the sustenance of those at the end of their lives through the fruits of the labour of those in the middle of their lives. In this chapter, I shall explain how such pensions can provide fair terms of cooperation that respect both the freedom and the equality of different members of society over time. I shall also explain how such pensions can figure in the realization of the Rawlsian ideal of a property-owning democracy.

Freedom

In a document entitled 'Freedom and Choice in Pensions', the then Chancellor of the UK Exchequer voiced the following appeal to 'pension freedoms' that resonates with many on the right:

> This government believes in the principle of freedom. Individuals who
> have worked hard and saved responsibly throughout their adult life
> should be trusted to make their own decisions with their pension

[1] *Political Liberalism*, p. 3.

How to Pool Risks across Generations: The Case for Collective Pensions. Michael Otsuka, Oxford University Press.
© Michael Otsuka 2023. DOI: 10.1093/oso/9780198885962.003.0005

savings ... [Therefore], individuals from the age of 55 with a defined contribution pension will be able to access their entire pension flexibly if they wish. Annuities will remain the right product for some, but I believe that people should be free to make their own choice about how to use their savings.... I want as many people as possible to be able to access their pension flexibly.[2]

Is there a good case, based on the values of freedom and flexibility of choice, for employers to provide their employees with options beyond enrolment in a collective defined benefit (DB) or collective defined contribution (CDC) pension scheme of the sort discussed in Chapters 1–2? In particular, should they provide workers with the options to invest in an individual defined contribution (IDC) scheme instead of, or as well as, a collective scheme, along with all of the former Chancellor's pension freedoms to convert or cash in one's pension pot? The answer is 'No' if these options encompass an inalienable and unconditional liberty to withdraw from the collective scheme by, for example, cashing in and withdrawing the monetary value of one's per capita share of the collective fund at point of retirement. Such an inalienable right is really a *restriction* on the freedom of workers to bind themselves on terms of their own choosing that will make them better off collectively. It is, in fact, contrary to the free-market values that champions of pension freedoms profess, as it prevents workers from making primarily self-regarding choices more effectively. Collective pension schemes are not collectivist *rather than* individualistic. They are both: a mutual society into which each individual voluntarily associates and thereby binds himself.

In order to realize intergenerational investment risk pooling, it will be necessary to take steps to ensure that the collective pension scheme remains stable on an ongoing basis, with a steady influx of new members. Suppose that workers had the aforementioned freedom to opt out of a collective pension scheme without financial penalty whenever collectivization would be less advantageous than what they could reap if they remove their per capita share from the collective scheme and invest it on

---

[2] Osborne, 'Foreword', p. 3.

their own. Such freedom to defect would threaten the gains of risk pooling for at least the following two reasons. First, the effectiveness of the collective scheme in pooling longevity risk would be undermined. By the time they retire, people will have a better idea of their life expectancy than they did when they entered the pension scheme as young adults, since they will know how healthy they have managed to remain over the past several decades of their working lives. Those who know at that point that they are likely to live longer than average will have more of an incentive to receive a pension from the collective scheme than those who know that they are likely to live shorter on average, the latter of whom will have more reason to withdraw their per capita share and draw it down individually, if they are permitted to do so. The long-lived might not, however, have enough to generate sufficient pension income if they pool only among themselves. A second reason why an inalienable right to withdraw and cash in one's per capita share at retirement would undermine a collective scheme is that it would render it less effective in pooling investment risk. People who reach the age at which they would like to retire when the stock market is high or when annuities on the insurance market are relatively inexpensive will have an incentive to withdraw their per capita share from the collective scheme at that point. That will make it more difficult to effectively pool risks only among those who remain in the scheme. Rather, one needs to pool risks between a larger mixture of the lucky and the unlucky. Steps, however, can be taken to stabilize a collective pension scheme without the need for a requirement of compulsory and permanent enrolment in it.

Without undermining risk pooling, workers could be provided with the freedom to choose or decline a pension on the following terms. They could be provided with the choice of entering into a collective risk-pooling option when and only when they *join* a pension scheme at the outset of their working life upon reaching the age of majority.[3] Having signed up, they would need to remain collectively invested from that point onward, or else pay a heavy penalty for withdrawing. At the outset, but *only* at the outset, they would also have the choice to invest entirely in

---

[3] Recall that the collective pension provision defended in Chapters 1 and 2 would take the form of a single, all-encompassing (society-wide) CDC or last-man-standing DB scheme.

their own private defined contribution (DC) pension pot, which provides them with complete freedom to cash in, or draw down, etc., when they retire. All this would be consistent with individual freedom, assuming, as one should, that freedom encompasses the right to bind oneself. In the case of Ulysses, such binding was necessary to protect himself against the indulgence of his imprudent impulses. Here, the binding would not be for the purpose of protecting individuals against such weakness of will. Rather, its point would be to prevent rational defections from a pension scheme that would destroy the cooperative benefit of risk pooling for the reasons sketched in the preceding paragraph.[4] Such binding therefore makes a valuable option possible which would not otherwise exist and thereby enhances the range of available options among which people can freely choose.

For the following reason, provision of such a limited choice to opt out of a collective pension scheme and go it alone would not threaten the viability of the collective scheme. At point of entry at the beginning of one's adult working life, each will be choosing under a fairly thick natural veil of ignorance regarding his or her own prospects for a long life and for a retirement when the stock market is bullish rather than bearish. Although people's known longevity risks differ at point of retirement, at this much earlier point of entry each person's known longevity as well as investment risks will be roughly the same as any other person's of a comparable age.[5] In large part because known longevity and investment risks are both significant and roughly equal at an early point of entry into the scheme, most will have compelling reasons of self-interest to damp down these risks, by means of their collective pooling into the DB or CDC scheme at this point, rather than going it alone via individual DC.

Recall that entry into the workforce upon reaching the age of majority will be the only point at which a person will be able to choose to join with others in pooling risks in a DB or CDC scheme. If a person instead opts, at point of entry, to go it alone via investment in his own DC pot, he will not have any future opportunity to collectivize his risks in a collective

---

[4] This is not, however, a classic many-person prisoners' dilemma, since it would not be rational for every single person to defect.
[5] This will be true at least insofar as the society in question is relatively just, rather than being riven by significant socioeconomic inequalities.

scheme. Most will therefore find it in their rational self-interest to enrol in the collective scheme at the outset, even though the cost of exit is high. Hence, there will be a sufficient number of people enrolled in the collective scheme to facilitate effective risk pooling and to sustain it over time.

The freedom complaint to which I have just responded mirrors a complaint regarding the inability to opt in and out of health insurance which is mandatory. The requirement that one can enter a collective scheme only at the outset, conjoined with a high exit penalty, is in order to prevent behaviour along the lines of refraining from purchasing medical insurance while one is young and healthy, and purchasing it only when one is older and in less good health. The so-called Obamacare mandate to purchase insurance when young and healthy is justified as a means of making possible a ban on excluding, or charging higher premiums for, those with pre-existing medical conditions and also making it possible to restrict the extent to which insurance companies are allowed to charge people higher premiums if they are older. If there were not something along the lines of such a mandate, such restrictions would give rise to a serious problem, whereby people purchase insurance only after they discover that they have an illness or disability that requires expensive medical care or where people refrain from purchasing insurance when they are young and healthy and wait until they are older and infirm. Were that to happen, risks would not be spread sufficiently thinly across a large enough pool, and premiums would skyrocket, thereby defeating the purpose of purchasing insurance.

Unlike the Obamacare insurance mandate, workers would not be required to enrol in a collective pension scheme on my proposal. Obamacare could and perhaps should be transformed in this direction, so that there is no longer a requirement to purchase medical insurance when young and healthy. Dropping this requirement would silence the objection against the insurance mandate that it is an unjustifiable restriction on freedom. Nevertheless, the purchase of insurance from the beginning of, and throughout, one's adult life could be made a necessary condition of protection from exclusion or much higher premium on the basis of pre-existing medical condition or advanced age. This is what is known as a continuous coverage requirement. The risk of not being able to take out affordable insurance later would provide each with a rational incentive to purchase health insurance from the outset.

The ban on discrimination against those with a pre-existing condition, or who are elderly, is conditional on their having maintained continuous coverage in the past. This makes explicit the implicit rationale for the Obamacare mandate, in a manner that silences the objection that the latter is an infringement on freedom. Everyone is free to opt out of continuous coverage. However, one then loses the sort of protection for having a pre-existing condition, or against age-based discrimination, that is possible only if the risk pool of people paying insurance premiums includes a sufficient number of the lucky (i.e., those who are young and healthy) as well as the unlucky (those who are elderly and infirm). One cannot effectively pool risks only or mainly among the unlucky. If, moreover, one refuses to contribute while one is lucky, then one cannot coherently complain against losing affordable insurance when one is unlucky.

Equality

In the actual world of unequal income, collectively funded pensions that are proportionate to earned income would be an improvement over a status quo characterized by IDC pensions proportionate to similarly unequal incomes.[6] On account of the benefits of risk pooling and the transfer from those who would otherwise be richer to those who would otherwise be poorer that this involves, collective pensions would often be more egalitarian than the pensions that IDC would yield under the same employer and member contributions.[7] Collective pensions would tend to be worse than IDC for some of the unlucky who will die prematurely. They would lose out on the opportunity to bequeath their pension pot that IDC allows. But egalitarianism speaks against bequests. Collective pensions would also tend to be worse than IDC for those

---

[6] These remarks apply whether the funded pension is DB, CDC, or a notionally funded pay as you go (PAYG). My remarks in this section apply to all three types of pension.
[7] Given the declining marginal utility of money, the egalitarian effects of these transfers would be more pronounced when measured in terms of welfare rather than money.

whose investments would fare best under the latter, since their high returns would be transferred to the less fortunate when returns on investment are smoothed. But egalitarians should welcome such transfers. In comparison with IDC, a collective arrangement would also promote equality via a modest increase in the ratio of the income of the 'bottom 99%' to that of the 'top 1%'. This is because the average level of those in the bottom 99%, whose income is mainly earned, would rise under a collective pension via an improvement in the delivery of their pensions, but better pensions would make less of a proportional difference to the more largely unearned incomes of the top 1%.

Though they would generally constitute an improvement over IDC in the dimension of equality, collective pensions proportionate to income here and now would nevertheless fall short of the realization of egalitarian justice. Given the extent to which actual inequalities in income are explained by circumstances beyond the control of individuals, they would fail to realize a 'luck egalitarian' principle of pensions proportionate to incomes that are unequal if and only if these inequalities are traceable to people's responsible choices rather than such circumstances.[8] Insofar, therefore, as collective pensions are proportionate to existing earnings, their efficient delivery of pension income through risk pooling would at least mirror, even if not magnify, injustices in the actual distribution of earned income.[9]

In contrast to a typical occupational pension, some basic state pensions are largely sensitive to the number of years worked rather than the amount of money earned.[10] A pension whose level were sensitive to nothing other than number of years worked would perfectly capture the

[8] See Dworkin, *Sovereign Virtue*, ch. 2. In '*Sovereign Virtue* Revisited', Dworkin disowns the name 'luck egalitarianism', since he notes that his version of egalitarianism 'does not aim to eliminate gambles...from people's lives' (p. 107). Alive to this defect with the term 'luck egalitarianism', Peter Vallentyne calls the view 'brute luck egalitarianism', where 'brute luck' is Dworkin's term for unchosen bad luck. (See Vallentyne, 'Brute Luck, Option Luck'.) 'Option luck' is Dworkin's contrasting term for bad luck that traces to choice under known risk or uncertainty (e.g., gambles in a casino). I shall employ the term 'luck egalitarianism' as an abbreviation of the more accurate and informative term 'brute luck egalitarianism'.

[9] They would also mirror inequalities whose injustice are not readily captured by luck egalitarianism, such as the lower lifetime earnings of women arising from their devotion of greater periods of their adult lives to caring for others. See Anderson, 'What Is the Point of Equality?'

[10] See my discussion of the 'Beveridge approach' in the previous chapter.

luck egalitarian principle of choice-sensitivity under the idealized assumptions that the number of years one works is completely under one's control and the utility of labour per unit of time is the same across different people. These assumptions do not hold in the real world: some people lack a choice regarding years worked on account of involuntary unemployment or disability, and the disutility of low-paid jobs tends to be greater than that of high-paid jobs. A pension whose level were based only on years worked would, however, capture the choice-sensitivity of luck egalitarianism better than collective occupational pensions that are highly proportionate to earnings.

Insofar, therefore, as the imperative of equality is concerned, it will be difficult to make the case for collective occupational pensions proportionate to existing income as opposed to occupational pensions that are sensitive only to numbers of years worked. Alternatively, collective occupational pensions proportionate to income might be defensible only after one has realized policies that redistribute the underlying income itself, perhaps via a complex system of progressive taxation which ensures that this income is sensitive to one's choice but insensitive to circumstances beyond one's control.

In this section, I shall argue that an important element of justice is nevertheless captured by collective pensions proportionate to income, even when the distribution of income itself is not in accord with egalitarian principles. There is a justice-based case for collective pensions, because justice should be conceived of, not as fundamentally a matter of the elimination of the unfairness of unchosen, brute bad luck, but rather as fundamentally involving Rawlsian fair terms of social cooperation for mutual advantage in the division of the fruits of the labour of workers.

At its most fundamental level, the principle that constitutes Rawlsian justice is one of reciprocity. In particular, we do things to reciprocal advantage, on fair terms, where such terms are egalitarian. Recall that Rawls writes that

the idea of reciprocity lies between the idea of impartiality, which is altruistic (being moved by the general good), and the idea of mutual advantage understood as everyone's being advantaged with respect to each person's present or expected future situation as things are. As understood in justice as fairness, reciprocity is a relation between citizens expressed by principles of justice that regulate a social world in which everyone benefits judged with respect to an appropriate benchmark of equality defined with respect to that world.[11]

In rejecting the 'idea of mutual advantage', Rawls maintains that justice might call for the transformation of a present-day 'society in which property, in good part as a result of fortune and luck, is very unequal into a well-ordered society regulated by [his] two principles of justice'. Justice might call for such a transformation even if, as is likely, not all can expect to gain from it, relative to the inegalitarian status quo. Those, for example, 'owning large properties' can expect to lose 'greatly'.[12]

We can agree with Rawls that it is not a necessary condition of justice that all must be expected to benefit, relative to an unequal status quo. But this does not rule out the possibility of mutually beneficial moves from an unjustly unequal status quo that promote justice.

In the quoted passage, Rawls analyses reciprocity as fair terms of social cooperation for mutual advantage, as measured against a benchmark of equality. Both mutual advantage and equality figure in Rawls's idea of reciprocity. Each element has a role.

The very fact that Rawls describes equality in the distribution of goods as a benchmark implies that such equality does not exhaust justice. If, for example, there were no cooperation in a world where, as nature would have it, there were no unchosen inequalities among different individuals, we would have perfect luck egalitarian justice. But Rawlsian justice would be absent, as there would be no fair terms of cooperation that make all parties better off, when measured against a benchmark of equality. More generally, social justice would be absent in such luck egalitarian circumstances. Only natural justice would obtain.

Cohen's luck egalitarian case against the justice of strong Pareto improvements that do not promote equality might plausibly apply to benefits to all that are the result of brute natural forces: e.g., manna that falls from heaven.[13] But when the question is one of how to

---

[11] *Political Liberalism*, pp. 16–17.   [12] *Political Liberalism*, p. 17.
[13] See Cohen, *Rescuing Justice*, pp. 315–23.

distribute the fruits of the labour of socially cooperating individuals, considerations of justice might apply, which are absent in the natural case. A principle of 'to each according to his contribution', where what a worker receives is proportionate to the value of his labour contribution, has plausibility when applied to the distribution of the fruits of social cooperation from an equal baseline.[14] Such a principle is not, however, applicable, at least not in any obvious way, to the distribution of manna from heaven.

In addition to mutual advantage that arises from an equal baseline, there is another way in which equality might combine with mutual advantage to constitute fair terms of cooperation: mutual advantage might be realized among parties *who regard one another as equals*. Rawls refers to the benchmark of an equal division in the passage I have quoted. But elsewhere he often speaks of 'fair terms of social cooperation between citizens *regarded as free and equal*'.[15] These two conceptions of equality can come apart, in ways that bring out the importance of the latter, as I shall now illustrate.

It is plausible to maintain that a benchmark of equality should be choice sensitive: one involving equality of opportunity for goods rather than equality of outcome when the two come apart. Rawls himself is sympathetic to the idea that a Malibu surfer who has chosen not to work has received all the primary goods to which he is entitled in the form of leisure, even though he lacks enough material resources to sustain himself.[16] From a baseline of equality of opportunity, such a surfer might seek earnings from employment when his hunger becomes too great. It would, however, be unjust because exploitative for a capitalist to take advantage of the surfer's vulnerability by offering him sweatshop terms even if the transaction is mutually advantageous. The capitalist would not be showing regard for the surfer as an equal, but rather regarding him as someone to be taken advantage of, even though the exploitative transaction arises from a justly equal baseline.

---

[14] For an account of how 'to each according to his contribution' might be regarded as a principle which a suitably designed social contract would arrive at in such circumstances, see Weale, *Democratic Justice and the Social Contract*, chs. 3 and 7.

[15] *Justice as Fairness*, p. 79 (emphasis added).

[16] See Rawls, *Political Liberalism*, pp. 181–2 n. 9.

I have just argued that mutual advantage from the surfer–capitalist baseline of equal opportunity for goods needn't be just because it might involve failure to treat people as equals. I shall now argue that mutual advantage from an *unequal* baseline needn't be *unjust* because it might involve a regard of one another as equals in a manner that vindicates the transaction.

Among mutually advantageous moves from an unjustly unequal baseline, we should distinguish the following types of case:

1. The mutually advantageous move is *coerced via violation of negative rights*, as in the case of a gunman's money-or-life threat.
2. The mutually advantageous move involves an *exploitative offer that takes advantage of the vulnerability of the weaker party*. An exploitative sweatshop work contract in which the vulnerability of the worker is not chosen in Malibu-surfer fashion is one such example. Wage bargaining by the talented, of the sort that Cohen condemns in his discussion of the incentives argument for inequality, would also qualify.[17]
3. The mutually advantageous move involves neither of the above defects. It is *voluntary rather than coerced*, and *the stronger party does not take advantage of the weaker party*.

The move from IDC to the collective provision of occupational pensions is of this third type. It therefore counts as a case of genuine reciprocity even though it arises from an unjustly unequal baseline. Under a collective arrangement, each party voluntarily brings his pension contributions to the collective, risk-pools these resources with the resources of others, and then gets back in proportion to what he puts in. How much one is able to put in might be a reflection of an unjustly unequal baseline distribution of income. But the unjustly rich do not take advantage of, or otherwise benefit from, the fact that others are poor. Rather, insofar as their agreement is concerned, the positions of the different parties are symmetrical.[18]

---

[17] See Cohen, *Rescuing Justice*, ch. 1.
[18] As I discuss in the Appendix, however, there are different ways of rendering pensions proportional to income, some of which are more symmetrical in their treatment of the different parties and hence a better realization of reciprocity among those with unequal incomes.

Consider an analogous case in which a wealthy carpenter has constructed a sailboat without a sail and a poor weaver has weaved sails. They would each like to sell what they have produced. Suppose that the value of each sold separately does not add up to the value of the two together, given the synergy of their combination. If the poor weaver were desperate for the extra proceeds from the synergistic sale, perhaps the wealthy carpenter could drive a hard bargain for a disproportionately great share of these proceeds. That would be to take advantage of unequal bargaining power. By contrast, an agreement analogous to a collective pension is one in which they voluntarily split the extra proceeds in a manner that is proportional to the market value of each when sold separately. As in the sailboat case, the baseline for a collective pension is the value of what each owns when it is not joined together with what another owns: i.e., the market value of the assets in one's non-risk-pooled IDC pension pot.[19]

Here I am endorsing a principle which calls for each to receive according to his labour contribution. Marx famously rejected such a principle according to which 'the individual producer receives back from society ... exactly what he gives to it [and the] right of the producers is *proportional* to the labour they supply'. He dismissed this as a bourgeois notion that would be superseded: 'In a higher phase of communist society, ... after ... all the springs of co-operative wealth flow more abundantly—only then can the narrow horizon of bourgeois right be crossed in its entirety and society inscribe on its banners:

---

[19] Joseph Heath suggests a different interpretation of Rawls as judging occupational pension schemes just simply insofar as they have been voluntarily entered into in accordance with the law. Heath notes that Rawls claims that his principles of social justice do not apply to voluntary associations such as universities and business firms, which lie outside of the 'basic structure' of society. (See Heath, 'Contractualism', pp. 160–3.) But the questions of what sort of regulations should apply to collective pensions, and whether tax relief should be extended to pension contributions, seem clearly to be questions regarding the basic structure. Moreover, for reasons G. A. Cohen has offered, I would maintain that Rawlsian principles of justice ought to apply, far more extensively than Rawls thought they should, to the private choices of employers and employees. (See Cohen, *Rescuing Justice*, esp. ch. 3.) In discussions between union and employer regarding cuts to pensions or increases in contributions, considerations of equality, fairness (equity), and progressivity of effect figure prominently. Typically, however, the scope of these concerns is limited to the scheme membership and does not extend to those outside the scheme who are worse off. Perhaps this reflects the belief that there is a special requirement for terms of cooperation to be fair.

From each according to his ability, to each according to his needs!'[20] Leaving aside surfers and others who are in need by purely voluntary choice, we might acknowledge duties on the part of the better off to transfer resources to those in need, even when such transfers are not mutually advantageous. But when everyone has enough so that nobody is in need, the demands of equality need not always trump the strong Pareto improvements of mutual advantage when the two come into conflict. In these circumstances beyond the realm of needs, these two elements of justice—equality and mutual advantage—stand in a more equal relation to one another. A state pension should be sufficient to meet our basic needs for income in retirement. Above that floor, there is a sound case for the mutually beneficial risk pooling of a collective pension even if it arises from a baseline of unequal income.[21]

Property-Owning Democracy

In his 'Preface for the Revised Edition' of A Theory of Justice, which was published nearly thirty years after the original edition, John Rawls comments that, if he were writing the book now, he would

distinguish more sharply the idea of a property-owning democracy... from the idea of a welfare state. These ideas are quite different, but since they both allow private property in productive assets, we may be misled into thinking them essentially the same.[22]

Many state PAYG pensions conform to the idea of a redistributive welfare state that is characterized by ongoing transfers of income from one group of people in society to another: in this case, from those who are working to those who are retired. Collectively funded occupational

---

[20] Marx, 'Critique of the Gotha Programme', pp. 17–19.

[21] There is also the following pragmatic argument that we should not hold the aspect of justice involving mutual advantage hostage to the egalitarian aspect: the latter will be more difficult to achieve, since it involves a sacrifice of the interests of some, relative to the status quo, whereas the former does not. There is a case for not making the ideally just the enemy of the good.

[22] p. xiv.

pension schemes, by contrast, conform to the idea of a property-owning democracy, which Rawls endorses in preference to welfare state capitalism. Rawls maintains that

> the background institutions of property-owning democracy work to disperse the ownership of wealth and capital ... not [as in the case of welfare state capitalism] by the redistribution of income to those with less at the end of each period, so to speak, but rather by ensuring the widespread ownership of productive assets and human capital (that is, education and trained skills) at the beginning of each period. ... The intent is not simply to assist those who lose out through accident and misfortune ..., but rather to put all citizens in a position to manage their own affairs on a footing of a suitable degree of social and economic equality.[23]

Rawls expresses the hope that, in a property-owning democracy, 'most things can be left to citizens and associations themselves, provided they are put in a position to take charge of their own affairs and are able to make fair agreements with one another under social conditions ensuring a suitable degree of equality'.[24]

Collectively funded pension schemes would emerge from the choices of individuals and private associations to 'make fair agreements with one another' to pool their assets and share their liabilities in the form of mutual associations.[25] In order to secure a guaranteed pension income, workers would not therefore—as under contrasting and increasingly

---

[23] *Justice as Fairness*, p. 139.

[24] *Justice as Fairness*, p. 159. Considerations of autonomy along these lines were offered in favour of the setting up of a funded DB scheme among UK universities rather than seeking the sort of PAYG arrangement that civil servants and schoolteachers had. It was feared that the latter

> would ... transfer to a government department the powers and responsibilities of the trustees [of a funded DB scheme], and turn retired university teachers into pensioners of the state. Such an arrangement seems to us to have little advantage over the creation of a body of trustees with the powers we envisage ...
>
> (University Grants Committee, 'The Superannuation of University Teachers', p. 7)

[25] Here I extrapolate to the case of pension provision, as Rawls does not himself address the manner in which pensions might arise in a property-owning democracy.

prevalent arrangements involving individual DC retirement savings accounts—be forced to enter into a market exchange to secure a contract for an annuity from a profit-seeking insurance company whose shareholders are other than the workers in the collective. Rather, they would remain invested members of their own mutual association, with pension income paid out of the pooled resources of the collective throughout their retirement.

There would be no need to attract outside investors to start and sustain their pension schemes, whose members could instead draw upon the steady stream of small monthly pension contributions from workers and their employers. It would be a virtue to some, such as R. H. Tawney, who are associated with the idea of property-owning democracy, that the income-bearing assets in the pension fund derive, via such contributions, from labour income and in this respect are 'related to genuine productive effort'.[26]

In arguing that Rawlsian property-owning democracy unjustifiably minimizes the role of welfare state provision involving taxation and transfer, Ben Jackson writes:

if the major forms of individual property ownership that could plausibly be equalized in contemporary capitalist societies are home ownership and shares in private companies, then, as the financial crisis of 2008 has made clear, this will inevitably involve the exposure of individuals to significant financial risk. It is therefore crucial to secure individuals against such risks through collective social welfare provision if the property-owning democracy strategy is to be pursued.[27]

One of the main themes of this book, however, is that the mutual association of workers and employers, and the pooling of their pension contributions, is a means, beyond state transfers to the unfortunate, of protecting people against financial risk. Such risk pooling can provide a fairly high level of financial security even when pension contributions are

---

[26] See Jackson, 'Property-Owning Democracy', p. 41.
[27] Jackson, 'Property-Owning Democracy', p. 48.

invested primarily in stocks and shares, thereby allowing workers to share in the proceeds of the growth of the economy.

James Meade himself, from whom Rawls borrowed the very term 'property-owning democracy', called for something closely resembling the investment approach of a collectively funded pension scheme when he advocated 'the encouragement of financial intermediaries in which small savings can be pooled for investment in high-earning risk bearing securities'.[28] Pension funds are a means of spreading returns to capital throughout the population, as the inclusion of a greater number of ordinary workers among the beneficiaries of shares is achieved by the collective investment of occupational pension funds in shareholder equity. Large occupational pension funds dwarf even the endowments of Harvard, Yale, and Princeton. They allow workers of more modest means than the typical Ivy League graduate to reap the benefits, in retirement, of economies of scale and the greatest skill on offer for the management of the investments in their funds.

Funded collective occupational pension schemes involve a massive conversion of corporate wealth—the equities held in the scheme's fund—into income streams that take the form of annuities which provide for the retirements of workers. IDC pension pots, by contrast, involve the atomistic privatization rather than the collective sharing of corporate wealth, by providing people with lump sums of capital at retirement. By providing annuities rather than lump sums, collectively funded pensions reduce the scope for the rise of intergenerational inequalities through bequests of capital.

Collective, funded occupational pension schemes can also give rise to the voluntary provision of primary goods that the state would otherwise need to step in to deliver. Especially where there are political constraints on the raising of taxes or increases in government borrowing, we should attend to the full range of instruments at our disposal for securing such goods through the private firms and voluntary associations that form civil society. We should seek to facilitate those voluntary collective schemes that most efficiently convert the pension contributions of workers into income in retirement, without excessive

---

[28]   Meade, *Efficiency, Equality and the Ownership of Property*, p. 59.

profit taking by the wealthy through management charges and shareholder earnings. The less of his wage or salary a worker needs to set aside to generate a good pension, the more income from labour will be available for taxation for purposes of redistribution to the least advantaged, who thereby also benefit from the well-designed collective occupational pensions of others.

Conclusion

Why should those who are young, able-bodied, and productive agree to pay for the pensions of those who are elderly, infirm, and out of work?

Should they do so out of a duty to redistribute their known fortune to others who are known to be unfortunate, in order to eliminate the unfairness of life? If this is the answer to the question I have just posed, then we will have to rely on the capacity of the fortunate to identify with the fates of badly off strangers and altruistically agree to open their wallets to them. And if the fortunate will not agree, then we will need to find a Robin Hood who will rob from the rich against their wills, to give to the poor.

In this book, I have tried to show how we can conceive of the case for collective pension provision differently, as a form of reciprocity. This takes the form of cooperation between persons which is to the mutual advantage of each with regard to their prospects. We can conceive of the resources that pension schemes transfer, not simply as transfers between different people, but rather as transfers within the possible future lives of each individual: as transfers from one's more fortunate possible future selves to one's less fortunate possible future selves.

This case applies, along the following lines, to those who have recently reached the age of majority and are near the beginning of their adult lives, most of whom are now able-bodied and productive. Barring miraculous breakthroughs in medical technology or discovery of a fountain of youth, they will not remain so forever. Some of them will, tragically, become seriously incapacitated during their working years on account of illness or accident. For a few, the illnesses or accidents they suffer will be so serious that they will not survive into old age. The great majority of them, however, will make it into old age and reach a point when they are no longer able or willing to continue working. But they do not now know how long they will live in retirement or how well

How to Pool Risks across Generations: The Case for Collective Pensions. Michael Otsuka, Oxford University Press.
© Michael Otsuka 2023. DOI: 10.1093/oso/9780198885962.003.0006

any investments they try to save up during the next decades for their retirement would fare.

From the perspective of the beginning of their working lives, it is therefore rational for each of them to enter into an agreement with others, who also do not yet know their fates, that, if one turns out to be among the unfortunate whose private pension pots would not have yielded enough for one's retirement, one will receive much more in retirement, whereas those whose pension pots would have overflowed their retirements will receive somewhat less. But this arrangement will work only if each agrees to bind oneself in advance so that, if one turns out to be among the fortunate, one is not allowed to defect from the scheme and go it alone. It is rational for each to agree to share one another's fates by pooling risks across both space and time, on fair terms of social cooperation for mutual advantage.

How Should Pensions and Contributions be Linked to Salary?

In this appendix, I shall address the following question: what relation, if any, should one's pension, and one's contributions towards it, bear to one's salary? First, I shall address this question from the standpoint of the rational self-interest of the worker who receives the pension. Then I shall address it from the standpoint of fairness between persons, among other impartial considerations of public policy.

Rational Self-interest

One has the following reason to strive for a relation of equality between one's pre-retirement and post-retirement income. On account of the diminishing marginal utility of resources, one has reason to consume the same, rather than variable, amounts of resources per year: i.e., to smooth one's consumption. Hence, *other things equal*, more equally distributed income over one's lifetime will yield more overall utility than more variable lifetime income.

We must, however, consider the various other things that are not in fact equal, to determine whether one has decisive reason, all things considered, to aim to bring one's post-retirement income up to the same level as one's pre-retirement income. Prime among the other things that are not equal is the ease and cost of making income available to spend in one's retirement rather than one's working years.[1] As was discussed in Chapter 1, it is a financial challenge to ensure that one has a steady and guaranteed income throughout the period of one's retirement, let alone one that is equal to one's pre-retirement income. Longevity risk—lack of foreknowledge of the number of years one will live in retirement—poses one such challenge. But even if one knew precisely how many years one will live in retirement, there would remain the financial difficulty and risk of investing in a manner that prevents the erosion of the purchasing power of the income whose spending one defers by saving it for retirement. There is an intrapersonal trade-off between equality among the temporal slices of one's life, on the one hand, and efficiency, on the other hand. Even, therefore, if one does not engage in any pure time discounting of the value of one's future years,

---

[1] It is also the case that one's needs and preferences to consume, and hence one's expenses, will not be equal throughout one's working years and the years of one's retirement. The raising of children during one's working years will give rise to significant variation in annual expenses at different stages of a career. Expenses related to leisure and medical and caring needs arise at different stages of retirement.

the cost of mitigating longevity and investment risk will tell in favour of spending one's income now rather than deferring this until retirement. These costs will often justify aiming for income in retirement that falls short of parity with one's pre-retirement income.

I have been implicitly assuming, in the above discussion, that among the things held equal are the level of one's pre-retirement salary throughout the years of one's working career. That is typically not the case. Especially for someone with a university degree, income tends to rise in real terms over the course of one's career.[2]

The benefit of a defined benefit (DB) pension has traditionally been specified as a proportion of one's final salary just before retirement. In recent years, however, there has been a shift to a specification of such a benefit as a proportion of one's *career average* salary, with revaluation for inflation, also known as 'CARE', for 'career average revalued earnings'. The following is an illustration of the difference between these two arrangements. In a typical final salary scheme, one is promised an annual pension income consisting of a specific proportion of one's final salary—such as 1/80th of that salary—in exchange for the contributions a member and employer pay throughout a given year of work. Someone who works and pays pension contributions for forty years would therefore receive a pension worth half (40/80ths) of one's final salary upon retirement. By contrast, in a typical CARE scheme, for each year of work in which contributions are paid, one is promised a pension consisting of a specified proportion (e.g., 1/60th) of the salary one has earned that year, but with upward revaluation of that salary in line with inflation during the years leading up to retirement. The upshot of this arrangement is that someone who worked and contributed for forty years would receive a pension worth two-thirds of career average salary in real (i.e., inflation-adjusted) terms, upon retirement.

What reason might an individual have to prefer a pension defined as a proportion of one's final as opposed to one's career average salary, other things equal? Among the things that tend to be unequal are the fact that a typical worker's final salary will be higher than his or her career-average salary. Let us adjust for that difference by stipulating that the sum total of pensions paid to all workers on a career average basis would be just as high as the sum total that would be if paid on a final salary basis.[3] In that case, whether it is in the rational self-interest of someone to prefer the one arrangement to the other will come down to whether one expects one's annual income to rise over the course of one's career and therefore to be higher at the end than on average, or one expects one's annual income to remain flat or else to decline in real terms over one's career.

---

[2] See Kong and Ravikumar, 'Earnings Growth Over a Lifetime'.

[3] In all my subsequent comparisons of final salary with CARE, it will be assumed that the sum total of pensions paid out to all members is the same in the aggregate. Hence, there will be a higher CARE accrual rate to compensate for the fact that, when one averages across the whole population of scheme members, the career average salary is typically lower than the final salary. It is for this reason that, in my example in the previous paragraph, I have chosen a 1/60th CARE accrual rate which is higher than the 1/80th final salary accrual rate.

Fairness and Efficiency

The answer to the question of whether a DB pension should be based on final or career average salary turns on the fairness of favouring those whose salaries rise throughout their careers over those with flat or declining salaries. It also turns on considerations of efficiency. In this section, I shall discuss these considerations in turn, starting with the latter.

When a pension promise is a defined proportion of career average salary, the liability is far more predictable than one that is a defined portion of the final salary. Throughout every year of a worker's career apart from the final year, one will almost always have more information regarding that worker's career average salary as compared with the final salary. Moreover, pension contributions that are specified, as they traditionally are, as a fixed percentage of a worker's annual salary will automatically provide a better match with that person's career average salary than they will of the final salary. They will do so for the simple reason that these contributions are set as a fixed proportion of that member's career average salary, at least in nominal terms. The move from final salary to CARE is therefore a means of de-risking a pension scheme, by more closely matching the defined benefits that constitute the pension liabilities to the assets that are purchased from contributions. Unlike a shift from equities into bonds to bring the assets into closer match with the liabilities, this form of de-risking does not require an increase in contributions to deliver a given aggregate sum of pension payments.

In addition to being more efficient for the reason just mentioned, CARE lacks a regressive feature of final salary, which favours those with relatively steeply upwardly sloping salaries throughout their career rather than flat or downwardly sloping salaries in real terms, where those with rising salaries also tend to be better paid than the latter. A final salary arrangement therefore redistributes from the poor to the rich. While CARE cancels such upwards redistribution, it does not go so far as to reverse the upward flow and redistribute downward from rich to poor. Rather, CARE pensions preserve the actual distribution of income, however unequal. For this reason, CARE provides a better solution than final salary to the problem I identified in the section of Chapter 4 on equality, since it provides a fairer and more reciprocal division of the mutual advantages that arise from a baseline of unequal salaries.

In its typical form, however, involving a flat rate of contribution as a fixed percentage of one's salary irrespective of whether the salary is earned early or late in one's career, a funded CARE pension suffers from a bias against younger workers who are a greater number of years away from retirement. Early career workers overpay for their pension in comparison with workers later in their career, as can be illustrated with the above example of a CARE promise of 1/60th of the salary one earns each year, in exchange for contributions which are the same fixed percentage of one's salary throughout one's career. Recall that the pension promise one receives in a given year is revalued for inflation during all subsequent years leading up to retirement. In a funded scheme, a member's pension contributions for that year's promise will be invested in financial assets during the period leading up to that member's retirement. If, as one should hope and as is typically the case, the long-term returns on these investments exceed the rate of inflation, then those early in their career make contributions that more than fully fund the pensions they receive in exchange for these contributions, whereas those late in their careers make contributions that less than fully fund the pensions they receive in exchange for these contributions.[4]

This bias would be cancelled out in the manner of swings and roundabouts if everyone remained in the scheme throughout equally long careers. However, not all do, and this arrangement is to the detriment of those who spend only the early portion of their careers within the scheme, in comparison with those who remain within the scheme throughout their working lives or are in it only during the latter part of their careers.[5] Such detriment does not constitute age discrimination. It is not essentially or necessarily a transfer from young to old. Rather, it is a transfer from those who end up with a lower average career age in the scheme to those who end up with a higher average career age. Those who receive such transfers might be younger in age than those who make such transfers.

Conventional age-insensitive $1/x$ DB accrual in exchange for contributions of a fixed percentage of salary is equitable for many under a traditional funded final salary pension arrangement for the following reason: early career contributions that reap many more years of investment returns are balanced by the fact that these early career contributions are lower, relative to one's final salary, than late career contributions, in the case of those with a typically upward sloping salary trajectory. With, however, the shift from final salary to CARE, the carrying over of such a combination of age-insensitive accrual and a flat percentage rate of contribution has given rise to the aforementioned problem of overpayment for one's pension early in one's career, in comparison with late career.

This problem can and should be rectified as follows. A funded CARE pension should abandon the setting of the member contribution rate as a flat and fixed percentage of salary for each year of pension accrual, irrespective of how far away from retirement. Rather, these contributions should be adjusted to take account of the rate and number of years of expected returns on the assets into which these contributions are invested. Members who are farther away from retirement should pay less for their $1/x$ CARE accrual, given that the best estimate of returns on the assets will be greater than the revaluation of their $1/x$ accrual for inflation. This would amount to the replacement of a flat member contribution rate with an actuarially fair

---

[4] At any given point in time, those who are a greater number of years from the normal retirement age will have been born later than those who are nearer retirement age. Moreover, the members of cohorts that are born later will generally have a longer life expectancy than those born earlier. This fact will partially mitigate their overpayment described in the main text of this chapter, as they will be paying for a greater number of years during which they can be expected to draw a pension. Even if, however, long-term investment returns only modestly outperform inflation, this increased longevity will fail to entirely mitigate the overpayment due to returns on investment. Moreover, increased longevity is typically at least partially adjusted for by an increase in the age at which one is eligible to draw a full pension.

[5] Hence, in the case of the Universities Superannuation Scheme (USS), early career researchers who fail to gain a permanent post are disadvantaged by CARE.

rate that is upwardly sloping as a percentage of annual salary, the closer one comes to normal retirement age. In addition to rendering things fairer for the reasons mentioned above, such an upwardly sloping member contribution rate would have the further benefit of lowering contributions for those earlier in their career, for whom it is generally more difficult to save for retirement, both because their expenses tend to be a higher percentage of their salary and because people temporally discount their more distant future to a greater degree.

References

American Academy of Actuaries, 'Measuring Pension Obligations' (November 2013). https://www.actuary.org/sites/default/files/files/IB_Measuring-Pension-Obligations_Nov-21-2013.pdf

Anderson, Elizabeth, 'What Is the Point of Equality?', *Ethics* 109 (1999): 287–337.

Arends, Matthew, Ruth Turnock, and Andy Harding, 'Collective DC—Stability and Fairness' (Aon, September 2015). https://www.aon.com/getmedia/de702f58-e6c9-48f7-a027-ad7745e815e4/Collective-DC-Stability-and-Fairness-final-final.aspx

Baker, Mark, and John Adams, 'Approaching the Endgame: The Future of Defined Benefit Pension Schemes in the UK' (Pensions Policy Institute, October 2019). https://www.pensionspolicyinstitute.org.uk/media/3311/20191029-db-endgame-report-final.pdf

Barr, Nicholas, *The Welfare State as Piggy Bank* (Oxford University Press, 2001).

Barr, Nicholas, *The Economics of the Welfare State*, 6th ed. (Oxford University Press, 2020).

Barr, Nicholas, and Peter Diamond, *Better Pension Design* (Oxford University Press, forthcoming).

Barry, Brian, *Theories of Justice*, vol. I (University of California Press, 1989).

Bernhardt, Thomas, and Catherine Donnelly, 'Quantifying the Trade-off between Income Stability and the Number of Members in a Pooled Annuity Fund', *ASTIN Bulletin: The Journal of the IAA* 51 (2021): 101–30.

Binmore, Ken, *Natural Justice* (Oxford University Press, 2005).

Blake, David, *Pension Schemes and Pension Funds in the United Kingdom*, 2nd ed. (Oxford University Press, 2003).

Bodie, Zvi, 'Mismatch Risk, Government Guarantees, and Financial Instability: The Case of the U.S. Pension System', *International Journal of Central Banking* 8 (supplement 1) (2012): 273–83.

Brown, Jeffrey, and George Pennacchi, 'Discounting Pension Liabilities: Funding versus Value', *Journal of Pension Economics and Finance* 15 (2016): 254–84.

Brown, Robert, and Craig McInnes, 'Shifting Public Sector DB Plans to DC: The Experience so far and Implications for Canada' (Canadian Public Pension Leadership Council, October 2014). https://cpplc.ca/wp-content/uploads/2018/01/db-vs-dc_plans_research-paper_2015-errata.pdf

Cannon, Edward, and Ian Tonks, 'The Value and Risk of Defined Contribution Pension Schemes: International Evidence', *Journal of Risk and Insurance* 80 (2013): 95–119.

Cohen, G. A., *Rescuing Justice and Equality* (Harvard University Press, 2008).

Cui, Jiajia, Frank de Jong, and Eduard Ponds, 'Intergenerational Risk Sharing within Funded Pension Schemes', *Journal of Pension Economics and Finance* 10 (2011): 1–29.

DeWitt, Larry, 'Details of Ida May Fuller's Payroll Tax Contributions' (Social Security Administration, July 1996). https://www.ssa.gov/history/idapayroll.html

Donnelly, Catherine, 'Pooling Pensioners' Resources', *The Actuary* (August 2018). https://www.theactuary.com/features/2018/08/2018/07/31/pooling-pensioners-resources

Dworkin, Ronald, *Sovereign Virtue* (Harvard University Press, 2000).

Dworkin, Ronald, '*Sovereign Virtue* Revisited', *Ethics* 113 (2002): 106–43.

Dworkin, Ronald, *Justice for Hedgehogs* (Harvard University Press, 2011).

Exley, C. J., S. J. B. Mehta, and A. D. Smith, 'The Financial Theory of Defined Benefit Pension Schemes', *British Actuarial Journal* 3 (1997): 835–966.

Faculty and Institute of Actuaries, 'GN 27: Retirement Benefit Schemes—Minimum Funding Requirement', v.1.0 (6 April 1997). https://www.actuaries.org.uk/system/files/documents/pdf/GN27V1-0.pdf

First Actuarial, 'Report to the USS Paper: 2014 Actuarial Valuation' (November 2014). https://www.ucu.org.uk/media/6937/UCU-response-to-the-USS-consultation-on-factors-affecting-the-reported-level-of-scheme-funding-Nov-14/pdf/ucu_usstrusteeconsultationresponse_nov14.pdf

Galvin, Bill, 'USS Update', Universities UK Conference 2019 (Universities Superannuation Scheme, 11 September 2019).

Guo, Jeff, 'It's Sleazy, It's Totally Illegal, and Yet It Could Become the Future of Retirement', *Washington Post* (28 September 2015). https://www.washingtonpost.com/news/wonk/wp/2015/09/28/this-sleazy-and-totally-illegal-savings-scheme-may-be-the-future-of-retirement/

Hampton, Jean, 'Contracts and Choices: Does Rawls Have a Social Contract Theory?', *Journal of Philosophy* 77 (1980): 315–38.

Heath, Joseph, 'The Benefits of Cooperation', *Philosophy and Public Affairs* 34 (2006): 313–51.

Heath, Joseph, 'The Structure of Intergenerational Cooperation', *Philosophy and Public Affairs* 41 (2013): 31–66.

Heath, Joseph, 'Contractualism: Micro and Macro', in Joseph Heath, *Morality, Competition, and the Firm* (Oxford University Press, 2014).

Jackson, Ben, 'Property-Owning Democracy: A Short History', in Martin O'Neill and Thad Williamson, eds., *Property-Owning Democracy: Rawls and Beyond* (Wiley-Blackwell, 2012).

Johnston, E. A., 'The Comparative Value of Pensions', *Journal of the Institute of Actuaries* 109 (1982): 1–38. https://www.actuaries.org.uk/system/files/documents/pdf/0001-0038_0.pdf

Joint Expert Panel, 'Report of the Joint Expert Panel' (September 2018). https://www.ucu.org.uk/media/9523/JEP-report-September-2018/pdf/Report_of_the_Joint_Expert_Panel.pdf

Jordà, Òscar, Katharina Knoll, Dmitry Kuvshinov, Moritz Schularick, and Alan Taylor, 'The Rate of Return on Everything, 1870–2015', *Quarterly Journal of Economics* 134 (2019): 1225–98.

Jordan, Dearbail, 'Royal Mail to axe up to 10,000 jobs as losses rise', *BBC News* (14 October 2022). https://www.bbc.com/news/uk-63253687

Kong, Yu-Chien, and B. Ravikumar, 'Earnings Growth Over a Lifetime: Not What It Used To Be', *Regional Economist* (1 April 2012). https://www.stlouisfed.org/publications/regional-economist/april-2012/earnings-growth-over-a-lifetime–not-what-it-used-to-be

Krugman, Paul, 'An Insurance Company with an Army', *New York Times* (27 April 2011). https://archive.nytimes.com/krugman.blogs.nytimes.com/2011/04/27/an-insurance-company-with-an-army/

Lilleston, Randy, 'Last American to Collect a Civil War Pension Dies at 90' (AARP, 5 June 2020). https://www.aarp.org/home-family/voices/veterans/info-2020/last-civil-war-pensioner-dies.html

Logan, Douglas, *The Birth of a Pension Scheme: A History of the Universities Superannuation Scheme* (University of Liverpool Press, 1985).

Marx, Karl, 'Critique of the Gotha Programme', in *Karl Marx and Frederick Engels: Selected Works in Three Volumes*, vol. III (Progress Publishers, 1970).

Meade, James, *Efficiency, Equality and the Ownership of Property* (George Allen & Unwin, 1964).

Merton, Robert, 'The Crisis in Retirement Planning', *Harvard Business Review* (July–August 2014), pp. 3–10.

Novy-Marx, Robert, and Joshua Rauh, 'The Liabilities and Risks of State-Sponsored Pension Plans', *Journal of Economic Perspectives* 23 (2009): 191–210.

Osborne, George, 'Foreword' to 'Freedom and Choice in Pensions: Government Response to the Consultation' (HM Treasury, July 2014). https://assets.publishing.service.gov.uk/government/uploads/system/uploads/attachment_data/file/332714/pensions_response_online.pdf

Otsuka, Michael, *Libertarianism without Inequality* (Oxford University Press, 2003).

Otsuka, Michael, 'Equality, Ambition, and Insurance', *Proceedings of the Aristotelian Society* supplementary volume, 78 (2004): 151–66.

Otsuka, Michael, 'How to Guard against the Risk of Living Too Long: The Case for Collective Pensions', in David Sobel, Peter Vallentyne, and Steven Wall, eds., *Oxford Studies in Political Philosophy*, vol. III (Oxford University Press, 2017).

Otsuka, Michael, 'Oxford's and Cambridge's Role in the Demise of USS' (12 February 2018). https://mikeotsuka.medium.com/oxfords-and-cambridge-s-role-in-the-demise-of-uss-a3034b62c033

Otsuka, Michael, 'Appropriating Lockean Appropriation on Behalf of Equality', in James Penner and Michael Otsuka, eds., *Property Theory: Legal and Political Perspectives* (Cambridge University Press, 2018).

Otsuka, Michael, 'Does the Universities Superannuation Scheme Provide a Model of Reciprocity Between Generations?', *LSE Public Policy Review* 2 (2021): 1–6. https://doi.org/10.31389/lseppr.42

Otsuka, Michael, 'Fair Terms of Social Cooperation among Equals', *Journal of Practical Ethics* (in press).

Pension Protection Fund, *The Purple Book: DB Pensions Universe Risk Profile* (2021). https://www.ppf.co.uk/sites/default/files/2021-12/PPF_PurpleBook_2021.pdf

Pension Protection Fund, 'Investment Principles and Strategy' (retrieved 29 November 2022). https://www.ppf.co.uk/investment/investment-principles-and-strategy

Pensions Regulator, 'Code of Practice No. 3: Funding Defined Benefit' (May 2014). https://www.thepensionsregulator.gov.uk/-/media/thepensionsregulator/files/import/pdf/code-03-funding-defined-benefits.ashx

Pensions Regulator, 'Ten Key Points about the Employer Covenant' (August 2015). https://www.thepensionsregulator.gov.uk/-/media/thepensionsregulator/files/import/pdf/ten-key-points-employer-covenant-at-a-glance.ashx

Pensions Regulator, 'Defined Benefit Funding Code of Practice: Consultation Document' (March 2020). https://www.thepensionsregulator.gov.uk/-/media/thepensionsregulator/files/import/pdf/db-funding-code-of-practice-consultation.ashx

Piketty, Thomas, *Capital in the Twenty-first Century* (Harvard University Press, 2014).

Ralfe, John, 'Collective Defined Pensions Are a "Ponzi Con Trick"', *Financial Times* (15 June 2014). https://www.ft.com/content/b4711a2c-f225-11e3-ac7a-00144feabdc0

Rawls, John, 'Justice as Fairness: Political not Metaphysical', *Philosophy and Public Affairs* 14 (1985): 223–51.

Rawls, John, *Political Liberalism* (Columbia University Press, 1993).

Rawls, John, *A Theory of Justice*, rev. ed. (Harvard University Press, 1999).

Rawls, John, *Justice as Fairness: A Restatement* (Harvard University Press, 2001).

Ritholtz, Barry, 'Tackling the "Nastiest, Hardest Problem in Finance"' (5 June 2017). https://www.bloomberg.com/opinion/articles/2017-06-05/tackling-the-nastiest-hardest-problem-in-finance

Salt, Hilary, and Derek Benstead, 'Progressing the Valuation of the USS' (First Actuarial, September 2017). https://www.ucu.org.uk/media/8705/Progressing-the-valuation-of-the-USS-First-Actuarial-Sep-17/pdf/firstactuarial_progressing-valuation-uss_sep17.pdf

Schmelzing, Paul, 'Eight Centuries of Global Real Interest Rates, R–G, and the "Suprasecular" Decline, 1311–2018' (Bank of England, January 2020). https://www.bankofengland.co.uk/-/media/boe/files/working-paper/2020/eight-centuries-of-global-real-interest-rates-r-g-and-the-suprasecular-decline-1311-2018

Silcock, Daniela, 'DC Scheme Investment in Illiquid and Alternative Assets' (Pensions Policy Institute, March 2019). https://www.pensionspolicyinstitute.org.uk/media/3112/20190325-dc-scheme-investment-in-illiquids-high-res.pdf

Spiegelhalter, David, 'Why "Life Expectancy" Is a Misleading Summary of Survival' (22 September 2014). https://understandinguncertainty.org/why-life-expectancy-misleading-summary-survival

Treasury, HM, 'Consultation on the Discount Rate Used to Set Unfunded Public Service Pension Contributions: Summary of Responses' (April 2011). https://assets.publishing.service.gov.uk/government/uploads/system/uploads/attachment_data/file/190119/consult_discount_rate_summary_responses.pdf

Treasury, HM, 'Update' to 'The Discount Rate Used to Set Unfunded Public Service Pension Contributions' (April 2011). https://www.gov.uk/government/consultations/the-discount-rate-used-to-set-unfunded-public-service-pension-contributions

Treasury, HM, 'Public Service Pensions: Consultation on the Discount Rate Methodology' (June 2021). https://assets.publishing.service.gov.uk/government/uploads/system/uploads/attachment_data/file/996113/SCAPE_Discount_Rate_methodologyFD.pdf

Turner, John, Humberto Godinez-Olivares, David McCarthy, and Maria del Carmen Boado-Penas, 'Determining Discount Rates Required to Fund Defined Benefit Plans' (Society of Actuaries, January 2017). https://www.soa.org/globalassets/assets/Files/Research/Projects/determining-discount-rates.pdf

UK Parliament, 'Pensions Act 2004'. https://www.legislation.gov.uk/ukpga/2004/35/contents

UK Parliament, 'The Occupational Pension Schemes (Scheme Funding) Regulations 2005'. https://www.legislation.gov.uk/uksi/2005/3377/contents

Universities Superannuation Scheme (USS), 'Report by the Actuary on the Actuarial Valuation as at 31 March 1993' (January 1994).

Universities Superannuation Scheme (USS), 'Report by the Actuary on the Actuarial Valuation as at 31 March 1996' (March 1997).

Universities Superannuation Scheme (USS), 'A Technical Overview of the 2017 Valuation—Subtitled' (video presentation uploaded 15 May 2018). https://vimeo.com/269879578

Universities Superannuation Scheme (USS), 'Methodology and Risk Appetite for the 2020 Valuation: Technical Discussion Document for USS Sponsoring Employers' (9 March 2020). https://www.uss.co.uk/-/media/project/ussmainsite/files/about-us/valuations_yearly/2020-valuation/2020-valuation-discussion-document-final.pdf

Universities Superannuation Scheme (USS), 'A Consultation for the 2020 Valuation: A Consultation with Universities UK on the Proposed Methodology and Assumptions for the Scheme's Technical Provisions' (28 August 2020). https://www.uss.co.uk/-/media/project/ussmainsite/files/about-us/valuations_yearly/2020-valuation/uss-technical-provisions-consultation-2020-valuation.pdf

Universities Superannuation Scheme (USS), 'Actuarial Valuation Report at 31 March 2020' (30 September 2021). https://www.uss.co.uk/-/media/project/ussmainsite/files/about-us/our-valuation/actuarial-valuation—march-2020.pdf

Universities Superannuation Scheme (USS), 'Monitoring of the 2020 Financial Management Plan—March 2022' (30 May 2022). https://www.uss.co.uk/-/media/project/ussmainsite/files/about-us/our-valuation/monitoring-of-the-fmp—march-2022.pdf

Universities UK (UUK), 'UUK Representatives' Views on Progress of the USS Valuation Methodology Discussion Forum (VMDF)' (17 July 2020). https://www.ussemployers.org.uk/sites/default/files/field/attachemnt/VMDF%20-%20UUK%20Representatives%27%20Views%20on%20Progress%2017Jul2020.pdf

University Grants Committee, 'The Superannuation of University Teachers' (HMSO, 1960).

Vallentyne, Peter, 'Brute Luck, Option Luck, and Equality of Initial Opportunities', *Ethics* 112 (2002): 529–57.

Weale, Albert, *Democratic Justice and the Social Contract* (Oxford University Press, 2013).

Wesbroom, Kevin, David Hardern, Matthew Arends, and Andy Harding, 'The Case for Collective DC' (Aon, November 2013). https://www.aon.com/getmedia/a745af28-9106-4e25-a09a-bdf4f5ead150/The-Case-for-Collective-DC_update_2020.aspx

Willis Towers Watson, 'Analysis: How CDC Pension Levels Compare with Other Types of Schemes' (September 2020).

Wren-Lewis, Simon, 'Unfunded Pension Schemes and Intergenerational Equity' (5 June 2012). https://mainlymacro.blogspot.com/2012/06/unfunded-pension-schemes-and.html

XPS Pension, 'Project Bronze—Summary and Next Steps Paper v19' (12 July 2018).

Index

For the benefit of digital users, indexed terms that span two pages (e.g., 52–53) may, on occasion, appear on only one of those pages.